IN... ENTIRE SHOP... CIRCUIT-RATED FOR SUFFICIENT AMPERAGE

STOCK FIRST AID KIT WITH MATERIALS TO TREAT CUTS, GASHES, SPLINTERS, FOREIGN OBJECTS AND CHEMICALS IN EYES, AND BURNS

HAVE TELEPHONE IN SHOP TO CALL FOR HELP

INSTALL FIRE EXTINGUISHER RATED FOR A-, B-, AND C-CLASS FIRES

WEAR EYE PROTECTION AT ALL TIMES

LOCK CABINETS AND POWER TOOLS TO PROTECT CHILDREN AND INEXPERIENCED VISITORS

USE DUST COLLECTOR TO KEEP SHOP DUST AT A MINIMUM

WEAR SHIRT SLEEVES ABOVE ELBOWS

WEAR CLOSE-FITTING CLOTHES

WEAR LONG PANTS

REMOVE WATCHES, RINGS, OR JEWELRY

KEEP TABLE AND FENCE SURFACES WAXED AND RUST-FREE

WEAR THICK-SOLED SHOES, PREFERABLY WITH STEEL TOES

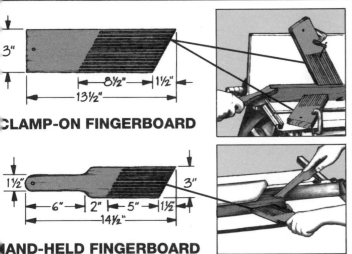

CLAMP-ON FINGERBOARD

3"

8½" 1½"

13½"

HAND-HELD FINGERBOARD

1½"

6" 2" 5" 1½"

3"

14½"

PROTECTION

WEAR FULL FACE SHIELD DURING LATHE TURNING, ROUTING, AND OTHER OPERATIONS THAT MAY THROW CHIPS

WEAR DUST MASK DURING SANDING AND SAWING

WEAR VAPOR MASK DURING FINISHING

WEAR EAR PROTECTORS DURING ROUTING, PLANING, AND LONG, CONTINUOUS POWER TOOL OPERATION

WEAR SAFETY GLASSES OR GOGGLES AT ALL TIMES

WEAR RUBBER GLOVES FOR HANDLING DANGEROUS CHEMICALS

THE WORKSHOP COMPANION™

MAKING BOXES AND CHESTS

TECHNIQUES FOR BETTER WOODWORKING

by Nick Engler

Rodale Press
Emmaus, Pennsylvania

If you have any questions or comments concerning this book, please write:
Rodale Press
Book Readers' Service
33 East Minor Street
Emmaus, PA 18098

About the Author: Nick Engler is an experienced wood-worker, writer, and teacher. He worked as a luthier for many years, making traditional American musical instruments before he founded *Hands On!* magazine. Today, he contributes to several woodworking magazines and teaches woodworking at the University of Cincinnati. He has written more than 30 books.

Series Editor: Jeff Day
Editors: Bob Moran
              Roger Yepsen
Copy Editor: Barbara Webb
Graphic Designer: Linda Watts
Illustrators: Mary Jane Favorite
              David Van Etten
Master Craftsman: Jim McCann
Photographer: Karen Callahan
Cover Photographer: Mitch Mandel
Proofreader: Hue Park
Indexer: Beverly Bremer
Typesetting by Computer Typography, Huber Heights, Ohio
Interior and endpaper illustrations by Mary Jane Favorite
Produced by Bookworks, Inc., West Milton, Ohio

Library of Congress Cataloging-in-Publication Data

Engler, Nick.
    Making boxes and chests/by Nick Engler.
        p.   cm. — (The workshop companion)
    Includes index.
    ISBN 0–87596–585–7   hardcover
    1. Woodwork. 2. Wooden boxes. 3. Cabinetwork.
        I. Title   II. Series:
Engler, Nick.   Workshop companion.
TT200.E64 1994
684.1'6—dc20   93–47386
                                                      CIP

    4 6 8 10 9 7 5 3   hardcover

Special Thanks to:

Rick Goehring
Gambier, Ohio

Gordon Honeyman
Tipp City, Ohio

Tom Lensch
Dayton, Ohio

Wertz Hardware
West Milton, Ohio

CONTENTS

TECHNIQUES

PROJECTS

TECHNIQUES

1

MAKING ONE-PIECE BOXES

Woodworkers have been building boxes and chests for at least five thousand years. For most of that time, they made them from a single piece of wood, digging out the inside to create a cavity. The reason was that until just 600 or 700 years ago, boards were extremely expensive — they had to be hand-sawn or rived (split) from logs, then smoothed with chisels and planes. A craftsman might spend more time making the boards than the box! Consequently, only the very rich owned furniture made from boards. Most folks simply found suitable logs and chopped or burned away the insides.

Lumber is more reasonably priced nowadays, and storage furniture made from boards has become the rule rather than the exception. However, craftsmen still make one-piece boxes. These are usually small projects, cut from a branch or a burl rather than an entire log. And instead of chopping or burning out the interior, we rely on one of three power tools to create the box cavity — a router, a lathe, or a band saw.

ROUTING BOXES

To rout a box from a single piece of wood, you must first cut the piece into two parts — one part will become the box; the other, the lid. Rout the box and the lid in two separate operations. First, cut away the waste inside the box to create a cavity, then shape the lid to cover the cavity.

ROUTING THE CAVITY

You can use any one of several router bits to cut away the inside of the box. The most common choices are a straight bit, a mortising bit, and a core-box bit. (SEE FIGURE 1-1.) In addition, you can use different routing techniques, depending on whether or not the bit is *piloted* by a built-in bearing.

> ### FOR BEST RESULTS
>
> **W**hen selecting a straight bit for cutting box cavities, look for one designed for *plunge routing*. On these bits, the flutes (cutting edges) protrude slightly *below* the body of the bit so they can be used for boring as well as side cutting. This makes it easier to rout a starter hole, then enlarge it to make the cavity. Some bits are intended *only* for side cutting. Their flutes are almost flush with the bottom of the bit, making it difficult to plunge the bit into the stock. Furthermore, these bits will burn the bottom of a cavity.

One of the easiest box-making methods is *pattern routing*. With a scroll saw or a saber saw, cut a plywood or particleboard pattern to the shape and size of the cavity you want to create. Slice the lid from your workpiece and attach the pattern to the box. Rout the cavity, keeping the pilot against the pattern as you cut the sides. (SEE FIGURES 1-2 AND 1-3.)

You can also rout a pattern with an unpiloted bit, but the technique is slightly different. Mount a *guide collar* on the base of your router and secure the bit in the collet so it protrudes through the guide collar. To accommodate the bit, the diameter of the collar must be slightly larger than the bit diameter. Because of this, the cutout in the pattern must be slightly larger than the cavity you wish to rout. How much larger? That depends on the sizes of the collar and the bit. Subtract the bit diameter from the collar diameter and divide by 2. The result will tell you how much bigger to make the pattern. (SEE FIGURE 1-4.)

Once you have determined the proper size of the pattern, the remainder of the technique is the same. Cut the pattern, attach it to the stock, and rout the cavity, keeping the collar pressed against the pattern as you cut the sides. (SEE FIGURE 1-5.)

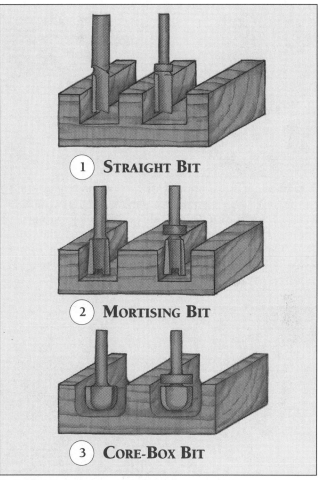

1 **STRAIGHT BIT**

2 **MORTISING BIT**

3 **CORE-BOX BIT**

1-1 Of the many router bits that can be used to cut a box cavity, the most common are the *straight bit* (1), *mortising bit* (2), and *core-box bit* (3). Each is available with or without *top bearings* — pilot bearings mounted on the bit shank, just above the flutes. (These bearings are usually the same diameter as the cutting diameter of the bit.) The routing technique you use will depend on whether or not the bit has a pilot bearing. **Note:** A straight bit with a top bearing is called a *pattern-cutting bit.*

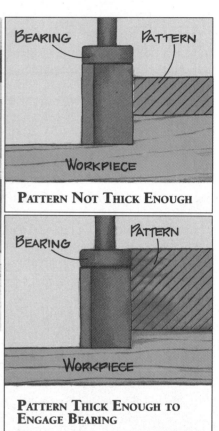

PATTERN NOT THICK ENOUGH

PATTERN THICK ENOUGH TO
ENGAGE BEARING

1-2 When using a piloted bit to cut the box cavity, first make a pattern to guide the bit. Cut the shape of the cavity in a piece of plywood or particleboard and sand the sawed edges smooth. (This pattern must be as thick or thicker than the length of the flutes on the bit. If it's too thin, the bearing won't engage the pattern when you make the first pass.) Attach the pattern to the wood you want to rout with double-faced carpet tape.

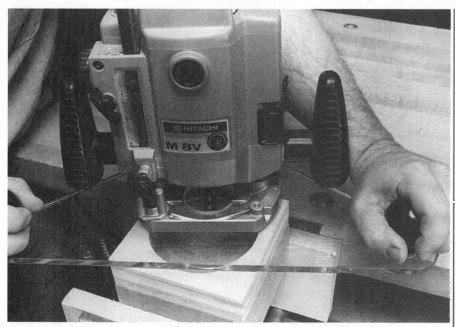

1 FEED ROUTER CLOCKWISE AROUND CIRCUMFERENCE.

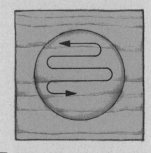

2 MOVE ROUTER BACK AND FORTH.

1-3 Rout the cavity in several passes, cutting just 1/8 to 1/4 inch deeper with each pass until you reach the desired depth. Begin by routing the circumference of the cavity, keeping the pilot bearing pressed against the pattern. Then move the router back and forth to clean out the waste in the middle of the cavity.

TRY THIS TRICK

If you wish to rout a deep cavity — deeper than the bit will reach with the pattern mounted on the stock — make the pattern in ¼-inch-thick layers. Hold the layers together with bolts and wing nuts. As you reach the maximum depth of cut, remove the layers one at time, starting with the middle layers. Remove the bottom layer last, then use the sides of the cavity to guide the bit.

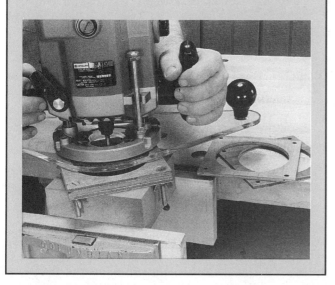

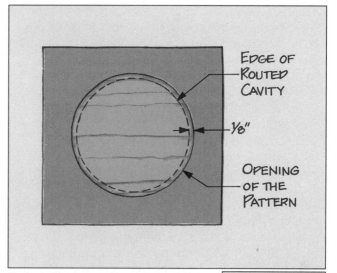

EDGE OF ROUTED CAVITY

⅛"

OPENING OF THE PATTERN

1-4 When pattern routing with an unpiloted bit and a guide collar, you must make the pattern slightly larger than the cavity you wish to rout. For example, if you're using a ⅝-inch-diameter guide collar and a ⅜-inch-diameter straight bit, subtract the bit diameter from the collar diameter and divide by 2, or

$$(\tfrac{5}{8} - \tfrac{3}{8}) \div 2 = \tfrac{1}{8}).$$

The pattern must be ⅛ inch larger than the cavity, all the way around.

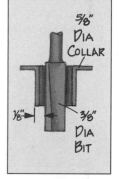

⅝" DIA COLLAR

⅛"

⅜" DIA BIT

PATTERN

GUIDE COLLAR

WORKPIECE

1-5 When routing the cavity with an unpiloted bit and guide collar, keep the collar pressed against the pattern as you cut the sides. Make the pattern slightly thicker than the height of the guide collar, so the collar doesn't rub on the work.

Finally, you can *pin rout* a box cavity with an un-piloted bit, using a stationary metal pin to guide the cut. Pin routing enables you to cut more-intricate patterns than other techniques. The recesses, corners, and other details in a pattern can be no smaller than the device used to guide the work — a large guide bearing or collar won't reach into a small recess. For example, when using a pattern-cutting bit, the smallest detail you can rout is 1/2 inch in diameter. When using a guide collar, it's 5/16 inch. However, when pin routing, you can cut corners and recesses as small as 1/8 inch, using a 1/8-inch straight bit and a 1/8-inch-diameter pin to guide it.

You can pin rout with either a router table or an overarm router. If using a router table, mount the pin directly above the bit. If using an overarm router, secure it beneath the bit. (The pin must be the same diameter as the bit and perfectly aligned with it.) Cut a pattern the same size and shape as the cavity you want to make. Attach the pattern to the work and place it under (or over) the pin. Keep the pin against the pattern as you cut the sides of the cavity. (*See* FIGURES 1-6 AND 1-7.)

ROUTING THE LID

There are two common types of box lids you can rout for one-piece boxes — *fitted* lids, which simply rest on the box, and *sliding* lids, which slide over the box.

You must shape the lid to fit the box opening. There are several ways to do this, each requiring different bits and different routing techniques. The simplest method is to cut a single rabbet in the lid. Or, cut two interlocking rabbets — one in the box sides and the other in the lid. You might also scoop out the underside of the lid to make a lip, then cut a rabbet in the sides of the box to fit the lip. (*See* FIGURES 1-8 THROUGH 1-11.)

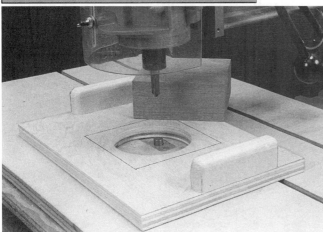

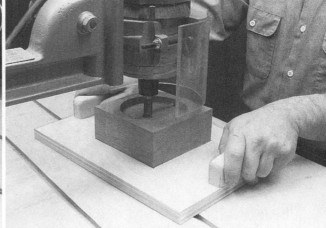

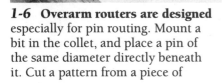

1-6 Overarm routers are designed especially for pin routing. Mount a bit in the collet, and place a pin of the same diameter directly beneath it. Cut a pattern from a piece of plywood or particleboard, and attach the workpiece to it with carpet tape. Adjust the depth of cut so the bit does *not* touch the work, and place the pattern over the pin. Turn on the router; plunge the bit into the wood; and rout the cavity, using the pin and the pattern to guide the work.

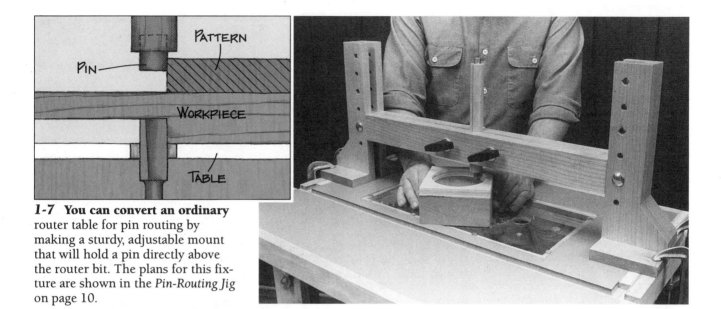

1-7 You can convert an ordinary router table for pin routing by making a sturdy, adjustable mount that will hold a pin directly above the router bit. The plans for this fixture are shown in the *Pin-Routing Jig* on page 10.

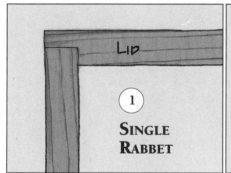

① **SINGLE RABBET**

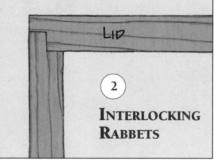

② **INTERLOCKING RABBETS**

③ **RABBET AND LIP**

1-8 Shown are three common ways to make fitted lids for routed boxes. The simplest is to cut a *single rabbet* (1) all around the circumference of the lid that fits the open-

ing of the box. Or, you can make *interlocking rabbets* (2). Cut a rabbet around the inside surface of the box, then rabbet the lid to fit the box rabbet. You might also make a

rabbet and lip (3). Rout a shallow cavity in the underside of the lid, creating a lip all around the circumference. Rabbet the outside surface of the box to fit the lip.

1-9 To cut a rabbet in a box lid, cut a pattern that fits the box opening. Attach the pattern to the lid with carpet tape and rout the rabbet with a pattern-cutting bit. The completed rabbet will fit the opening, centering the lid on the box. You can also use this technique to rabbet the outside surfaces of a box when the box walls are not a uniform thickness.

1-10 To cut a rabbet around the inside surfaces of a box, use a table-mounted router and a piloted rabbeting bit. This technique also works for outside rabbets, provided the walls of the box are a uniform thickness.

1-11 To make a lip in a box lid, you must cut a cavity in the underside as if you were making a shallow box. Here, a craftsman has used a pattern and a pattern-cutting bit to create a box lip.

TRY THIS TRICK

When routing a box with a simple rabbeted lid, the same pattern will make both parts, provided you are using either a guide bearing or a pin the same diameter as the bit. Cut the pattern with a scroll saw, using a fine blade so the kerf is as small as possible. (Don't make a starter hole; cut into the pattern stock from the edge.) Save both pieces — the cutout and the plug. Use the cutout to pattern rout the box cavity and the plug to make the lid rabbet. The two parts will fit perfectly.

To make sliding lids, cut interlocking joints in the lid and the box that slide together. The most commonly used joint is a sliding dovetail, made with a dovetail bit. (*See Figures 1-12 and 1-13.*) However, you can also make rabbet-and-groove joints with a T-slot cutter. (*See Figure 1-14.*)

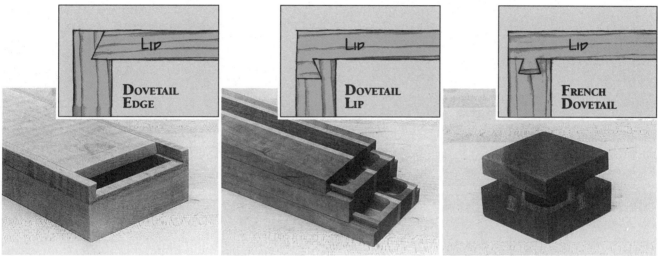

DOVETAIL EDGE

DOVETAIL LIP

FRENCH DOVETAIL

1-12 There are many ways to use a dovetail joint to make a sliding lid for a box. Shown are three possibilities.

1-13 Use the same bit to make both the dovetail groove and the mating dovetail so the angled surfaces of the joint mate perfectly. When routing a wide dovetail groove, remove most of the waste with a dado cutter, then rout the angled sides of the groove. This will save wear and tear on the bit.

1-14 You can also fit a sliding lid to a box with an interlocking rabbet-and-groove joint — rout the groove in the box, then rabbet the lid to fit the groove. Make both parts of the joint with a T-slot cutter.

PIN-ROUTING JIG

There are dozens of applications for pin routing in making boxes and chests. Not only is it a quick way to create small boxes, you can also use it to make trays and dividers for larger projects, carve finger-holds in drawer fronts, even hollow out secret compartments in legs and other components.

This fixture enables you to perform many pin-routing operations with an ordinary router table and a plunge router. The simple frame holds a pin over a router bit. The pins are interchangeable, allowing you to use different sizes and combinations of pins and bits.

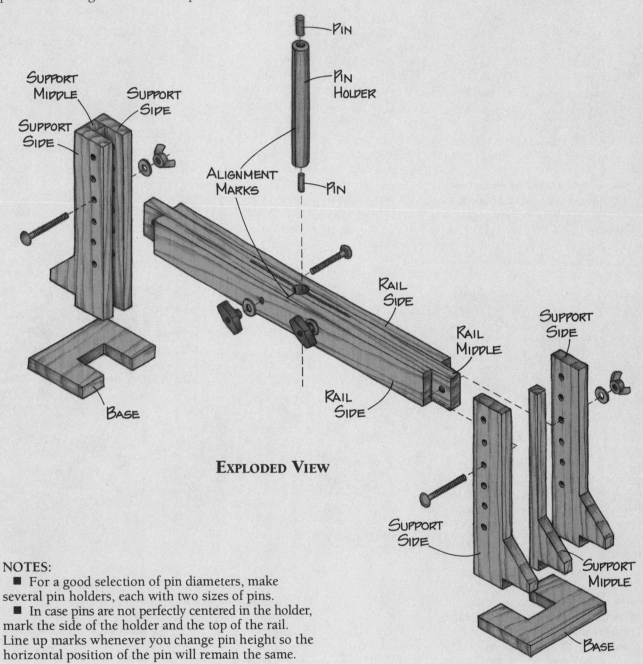

EXPLODED VIEW

NOTES:
■ For a good selection of pin diameters, make several pin holders, each with two sizes of pins.
■ In case pins are not perfectly centered in the holder, mark the side of the holder and the top of the rail. Line up marks whenever you change pin height so the horizontal position of the pin will remain the same.

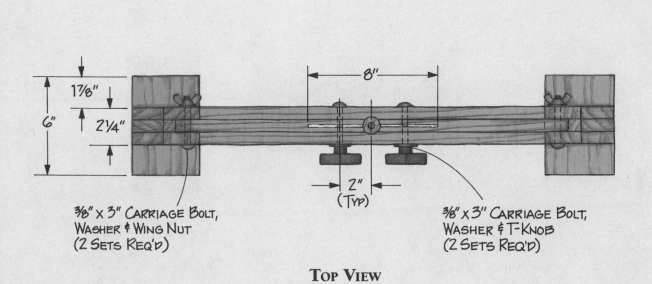

3/8" x 3" Carriage Bolt,
Washer & Wing Nut
(2 Sets Req'd)

3/8" x 3" Carriage Bolt,
Washer & T-Knob
(2 Sets Req'd)

Top View

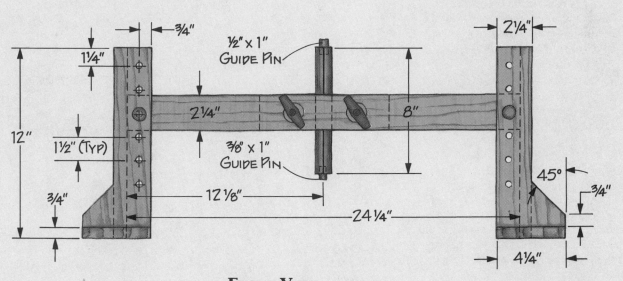

1/2" x 1"
Guide Pin

3/8" x 1"
Guide Pin

Front View

(continued) ▷

PIN-ROUTING JIG — CONTINUED

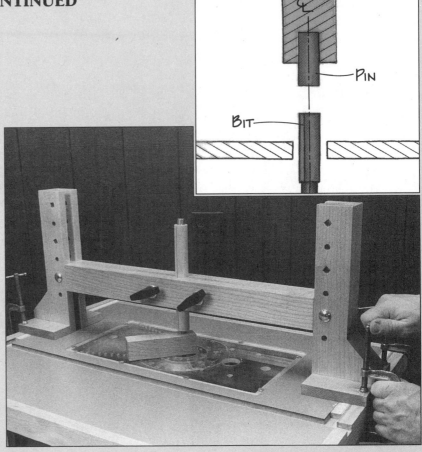

1   **The first step in any** pin-routing procedure is to align the pin with the bit. The center of the pin must be directly over the center of the bit for the cuts to be accurate. To do this, drill a hole through a scrap of wood to make an alignment block. The hole must be the same diameter as the pin and bit. Raise the bit about $1/2$ inch above the table and place the block over it. Position the bit over the block and lower the pin into the hole. Then clamp the jig to the edges of the router table.

2   **To start a cut, attach the** stock to the pattern with double-faced carpet tape. Adjust the height of the arm so the pattern and the stock will fit under it. Lower the bit beneath the table surface, and raise the pin above the pattern. Place the stock over the bit so the pattern is directly under the pin, then lower the pin until it rubs against the sides of the pattern. (There must still be room to lift the stock $1/4$ to $3/8$ inch.) Align the marks on the side of the pin holder and the top of the rail, then tighten the T-knobs that secure the holder in the rail.

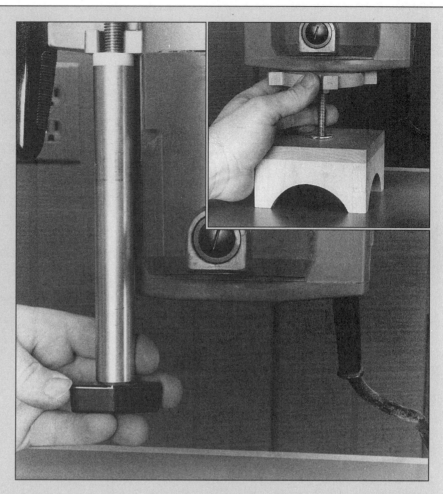

3 **Raise the bit ⅛ to ¼ inch.**
(This will lift the stock off the table slightly.) Grasp the pattern and hold it so the stock doesn't touch the bit. Turn on the router and lower the stock onto the bit. Rout the stock, guiding the cut with the pin and the pattern. Make deep cuts in several passes, raising the bit no more than ¼ inch for each pass. If the wood is very hard, you will get better results by raising the bit in ⅛-inch increments.

4 **You can also use this** pin-routing fixture for rabbeting and shaping operations. Here, a ½-inch straight bit and a ¼-inch-diameter pin are used to make a ⅛-inch-wide rabbet in a curved edge. By combining different sizes of straight bits and pins, you can create a wider variety of rabbet sizes than with a single rabbeting bit.

TURNING BOXES

You can use a lathe to make a box from a single piece of wood by turning the box shape, scooping out the interior, and fitting the lid. There are many ways to do this; turning is a highly individual craft, and every experienced turner has a favorite method. However, the basic box-turning procedure is a straightforward combination of simple techniques for turning spindles and bowls.

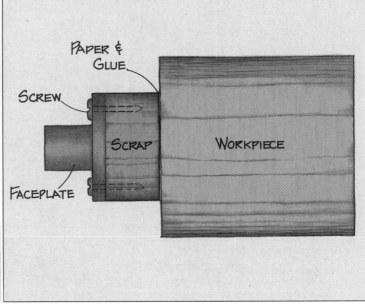

1-15 To turn a box, you must first mount the workpiece on the lathe. Flatten one surface with a disc sander or a belt sander and glue it to a thick scrap of wood with a single piece of paper between them. Attach the scrap to the faceplate with wood screws. The scrap prevents you from making screw holes in the workpiece, and the paper makes it easy to separate the workpiece from the scrap after turning the box.

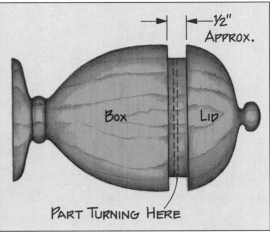

1-16 Mount the faceplate on the lathe and engage the live center — this will help stabilize the turning, especially if the workpiece is very large. Turn on the lathe at a slow speed and cut the outside shape of the box and the lid, leaving a ½-inch-wide space between the two. Turn the wood in this space perfectly flat, without any taper, and slightly smaller than the diameter where the lid meets the box. (This flat will form the rabbet on the underside of the lid.) Part the lid from the box so each piece retains some of the flat area. The lid should have most of it, but the box must have at least a tiny vestige to help you gauge the diameter of the opening.

Attach the workpiece to a faceplate, and mount the faceplate on a lathe. Turn the outside shape of the box and the lid, leaving them attached while you do this. When the shape is complete, separate the box from the lid. Scoop out the interior of the box as if it were a bowl, taking care not to cut the walls too thin. As you do so, enlarge the opening to fit the lid. (SEE FIGURES 1-15 THROUGH 1-19.)

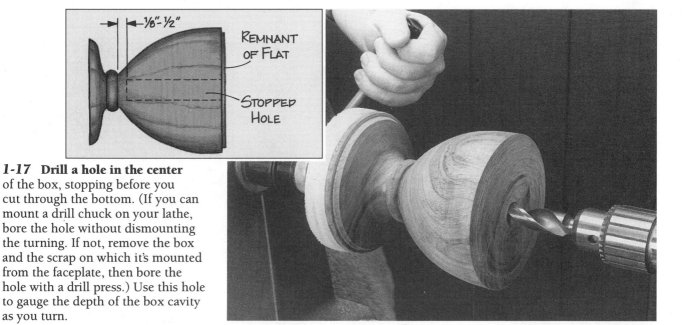

1-17 Drill a hole in the center of the box, stopping before you cut through the bottom. (If you can mount a drill chuck on your lathe, bore the hole without dismounting the turning. If not, remove the box and the scrap on which it's mounted from the faceplate, then bore the hole with a drill press.) Use this hole to gauge the depth of the box cavity as you turn.

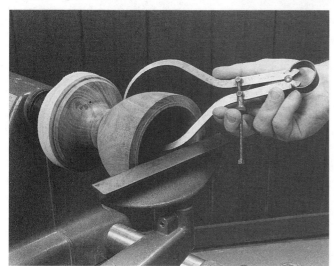

1-18 Create the box cavity by scraping away the interior. Be careful not to turn the walls too thin. Every so often, stop the lathe and gauge the wall thickness with calipers, as shown. Also be careful not to turn too deep. Place a pencil into the hole that you've drilled and put a mark on the bottom. Stop turning when you begin to remove this mark.

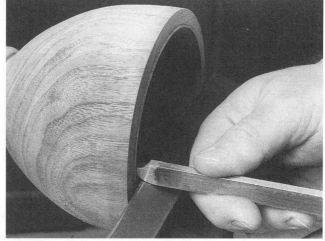

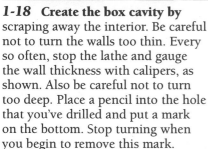

1-19 You can also use calipers to help gauge the size of the box opening when fitting the lid, but it's easier and often more accurate to use the remainder of the flat at the top of the box. Scrape away the inside surface of the opening until the flat is paper-thin. Then remove the stock *very* slowly (some craftsmen use sandpaper) until the lid fits snug, but not too tight.

Depending on the box design, you may wish to scoop out the interior of the lid. If this is the case, leave a substantial plug on the top end when you turn the lid. If possible, the end of this plug should be the same diameter as the flat space between the lid and the box. After separating the lid from the box,

mount the plug in a *lathe chuck* to hold the lid while you scoop out the interior. Remove the lid from the chuck, turn it around, and mount the flat (which now forms a rabbet on the bottom of the lid) in the chuck. Finish turning the shape of the lid, removing the plug as you do so. (*SEE FIGURES 1-20 AND 1-21.*)

1-20 To scoop out the insides of a box lid, you must leave a large plug on the top of the lid when you turn the shape. In some cases, it may be better to wait and turn the lid shape *after* it's parted from the box. Secure the plug in a lathe chuck and scrape away the stock inside the lid in the same manner that you hollowed out the box. Be careful not to cut away the rabbet or scrape away so much stock that the rabbet becomes fragile.

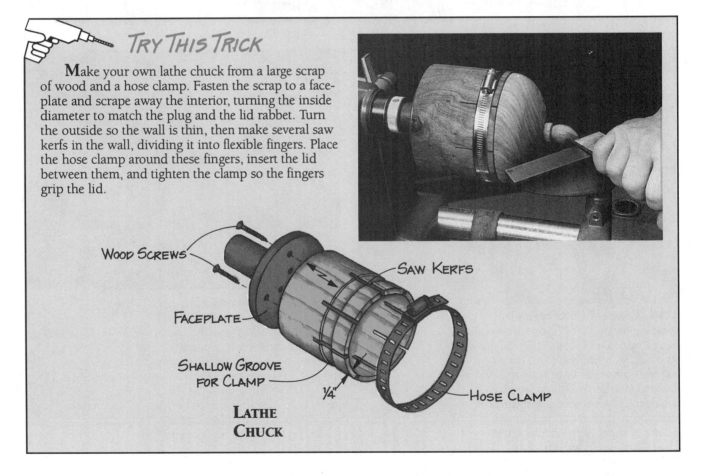

TRY THIS TRICK

Make your own lathe chuck from a large scrap of wood and a hose clamp. Fasten the scrap to a faceplate and scrape away the interior, turning the inside diameter to match the plug and the lid rabbet. Turn the outside so the wall is thin, then make several saw kerfs in the wall, dividing it into flexible fingers. Place the hose clamp around these fingers, insert the lid between them, and tighten the clamp so the fingers grip the lid.

WOOD SCREWS

SAW KERFS

FACEPLATE

SHALLOW GROOVE FOR CLAMP

¼"

HOSE CLAMP

LATHE CHUCK

1-21 After hollowing out the inside of the lid, remove it from the chuck. Turn it around and secure the lid in the chuck again. Finish turning the outside shape, removing the plug as you do so.

Band Sawing Boxes

To create a box from a single piece of wood on a band saw, cut the wood up into pieces, then glue them back together to form the hollow box and its lid. In essence, you are resawing the stock into smaller boards, then building a box from those boards. However, the boards must go back together in exactly the same position that they occupied before you cut them apart, so the grain on the surface of the box appears continuous.

There is no end to the number of ways you can cut up a chunk of wood and put it back together; consequently there are an endless number of box designs you can create on the band saw. You can make almost any shape you can envision with the right combination of straight, curved, angled, and compound cuts.

(*SEE FIGURE 1-22*.) The trick is to carefully plan the cuts, make them in the proper sequence, and label them so you can put them back together in their original positions.

1-22 With a band saw, you can create one-piece boxes of almost any shape by making the right cuts in the proper sequence, then gluing the pieces back together. The simple rectangular boxes were crafted by resawing a block of wood into small boards, making straight cuts only. The waste left over from each box was used to make the next-smaller box. The Noah's Ark is actually two boxes, the hull and the cabin. Each required a different progression of straight, curved, and angled cuts.

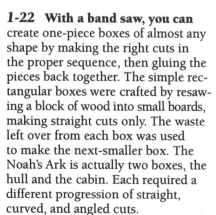

Here are just two possibilities — how to make a cylindrical box and how to make a box with drawers.

MAKING A CYLINDRICAL BOX

Although you can cut a cylinder from any piece of wood, this procedure is designed to make boxes from wood that is already roughly cylindrical — logs and branches. Let the wood dry thoroughly before you use it. Remove the bark and let the stock sit out of the weather in an *unheated* area for at least a year. Then bring it into your shop for three or four weeks so it reaches an equilibrium with the indoor environment. **Note:** If you don't dry the wood *and* acclimate it to your shop before cutting into it, the completed box will split or check.

Determine the top and bottom of the box, marking where you want to make the lid. Slice off the ends and cut away the interior to form the box cavity. Saw the lid free and glue the ends back on. After the glue dries, flatten the bottom of the box and attach the lid with hinges. (*SEE FIGURES 1-23 THROUGH 1-26.*)

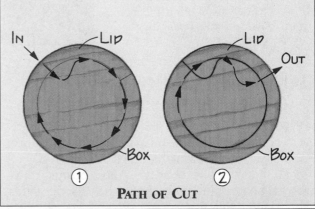

PATH OF CUT

1-23 To make a box from a log or branch, first cut off the ends with a band saw. Cradle the cylindrical stock in a V-jig to help steady and guide the wood as you cut. The slices you take off the ends should be about ½ inch thick.

1-24 Mark where you will cut the lid on the surface of the log, and how you will saw the cavity on one end. Turn the log so the marked end is up, and cut into the log at one of the lid marks. Following the marks that outline the cavity, cut away the interior of the box. Exit at the other lid mark. This single cut will create the box cavity and free the lid.

1-25 Set the lid aside. Glue the ends to the box, carefully aligning the grain so each end is in the exact same position it occupied before it was cut.

1-26 Let the glue dry, then joint or sand the bottom of the box flat. Sand the ends of the lid so it fits the box with a tiny gap at each end, and attach it to the box with hinges. Install a pull or carve a small depression in the front of the box just under the lid so you can lift the lid. **Note:** If you use a log with a protruding burl or branch, you can use this feature as the lid lift.

MAKING A BOX WITH DRAWERS

This band-sawed box with drawers is actually a miniature chest of drawers cut from a single piece of wood. The project shown has five drawers, but you can use this procedure to create a box with as many or as few drawers as you want.

Cut away the back of the box first, then the top, the sides, and finally the drawers and the dividers. Remove the drawers from the box front and slice off the drawer fronts and bottoms. Create the drawer sides and back by cutting the remaining parts in a

U shape. Glue the drawers together, and glue the back of the box to the front. When the glue dries, attach pulls to the drawers and insert them in the box. *(SEE FIGURES 1-27 THROUGH 1-30.)*

1-27 To make a band-sawed box with drawers from a single piece of wood, first mark the shapes of the drawers on the front of the workpiece. Cut off the back of the box, resawing the wood to make the back about 1/4 inch thick.

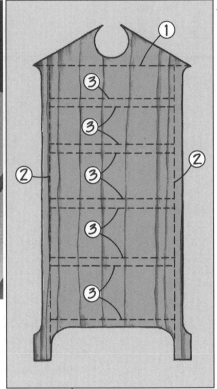

1-28 Cut off the top of the box (1), then the sides (2). Next, cut the drawers and dividers (3), as shown in the drawing. Use a ⅛- or ¼-inch standard blade and cut very slowly. This will give you the smoothest pos-sible cut surface and will help reduce the amount of sanding you'll need to do. *Don't* use skip-tooth or hook-tooth blades; they leave a rougher surface than a standard blade.

SEQUENCE OF DRAWER CUTS

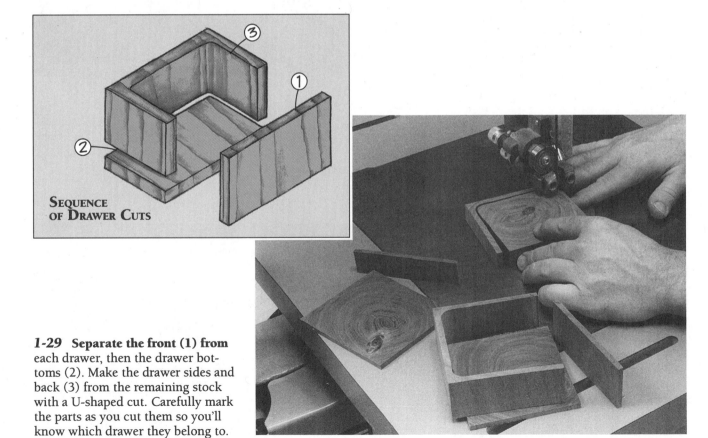

1-29 Separate the front (1) from each drawer, then the drawer bot-toms (2). Make the drawer sides and back (3) from the remaining stock with a U-shaped cut. Carefully mark the parts as you cut them so you'll know which drawer they belong to.

1-30 Lightly sand the inside surfaces of the drawers and glue the parts back together. Sand the sawed surfaces of the box parts and glue these back together. Sand the outsides of the drawers, insert them in the box, and sand the outside of the box. Do only as much sanding as is absolutely necessary; the more you sand, the sloppier the drawers will fit. If you wish, add pulls to the drawer fronts.

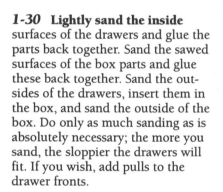

TRY THIS TRICK

If you want to, you can eliminate the drawer pulls by drilling *poke holes* in the back of the box. To open a drawer, poke your finger in a hole to push the drawer out.

2

MAKING SIX-BOARD BOXES AND CHESTS

The invention of the water-powered sawmill in 1328 caused a revolution in woodworking, including the ancient craft of making boxes and chests. Until that time, boards had to be rived or sawed by hand, and furniture was dear. If a person of modest means was lucky enough to own a chest, it was probably a dug-out log. But the sawmill made it possible for common people to own boxes and chests made from sawed lumber. *Joyners* (as medieval woodworkers were known) began to build storage units from just six boards — two sides, two ends, a bottom, and a lid.

The six-board box remains a practical and popular method of construction. Though simple, it is a remarkably versatile form. The best-known example is the traditional blanket chest; but lap desks, toy boxes, and tool chests are all variations on this theme. So are many smaller pieces, such as jewelry boxes, knife caddies, and cassette holders.

Box Joinery

Joinery isn't much of a concern when making a one-piece box, but once you begin building boxes and chests from multiple boards, it becomes paramount. Each joint must be at least as strong as the wood itself for the project to be useful and durable. Furthermore, the arrangement of boards and joints must allow for wood movement. Otherwise, the normal expansion and contraction of the wood will eventually tear the box apart.

ALLOWING FOR WOOD MOVEMENT

When building a six-board box, the wood grain in each board runs at right angles to the adjoining boards. Despite this, you can arrange four of the boards to move in unison without stressing the joinery. Traditionally, the *front, back,* and *sides* expand and contract in the same direction. (*SEE FIGURES 2-1 AND 2-2.*) Furthermore, the grain is oriented so the box opening will remain the same size as the wood moves. Because they move together, the front, back, and sides can be attached to each other with *rigid* joints — joints that are glued or fastened securely.

The other two parts — the bottom and the lid — must be allowed to expand and contract in a different plane. Typically, the bottom is captured in a *floating* joint — it rests in grooves or slots, but it's not glued in place. The lid may float also; other alternatives are to have it rest on a ledge or hinge it to the back. Any of these arrangements will work, provided the part can move without creating any stress.

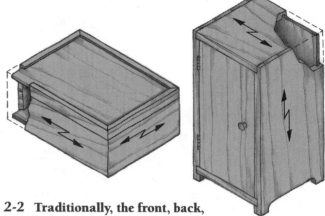

2-2 Traditionally, the front, back, and sides of a six-board box are rigidly joined, while the bottom and lid float. This doesn't have to be the case, however. You can build a box in which the top, bottom, and sides are rigidly joined, while the front and back are free to move. (Small cabinets are often made in this manner.) The box will be sound as long as (1) four of the boards move in unison, (2) these boards are rigidly joined at the corners, (3) their wood grain is arranged so the box opening remains the same size, and (4) the other two parts are free to move in a different direction.

2-1 This simple knife box with a sliding lid is a classic example of box joinery. The front, back, and sides are arranged to expand and contract in unison and are attached at the corners with rigid dovetail joints. The wood grain in these boards runs horizontally, and the boards move vertically — this way, the opening at the top of the box always remains the same size. The bottom and the lid are captured in grooves in the inside surfaces of the other parts. They do not move in the same direction as the sides and ends, nor are they held rigidly. Instead, they *float* in the grooves so they can expand and contract without stressing the box structure.

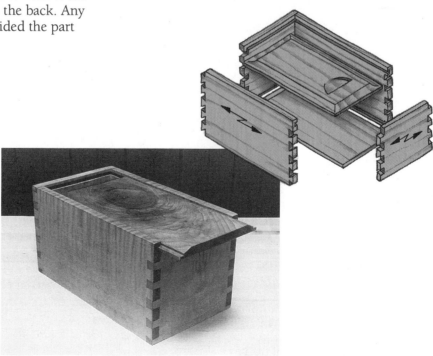

In addition to moving across the grain, wood has a tendency to *cup* in the direction opposite the annual rings as it gives up moisture and shrinks. (As it takes on moisture and swells, the cup will flatten out again.)

This movement may cause joints to gap at the corners if you don't plan for it. The rule of thumb is to join the boards of a box so the annual rings cup *out*. (SEE FIGURE 2-3.)

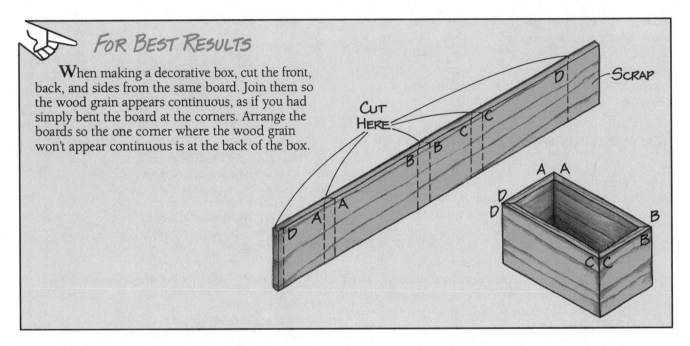

FOR BEST RESULTS

When making a decorative box, cut the front, back, and sides from the same board. Join them so the wood grain appears continuous, as if you had simply bent the board at the corners. Arrange the boards so the one corner where the wood grain won't appear continuous is at the back of the box.

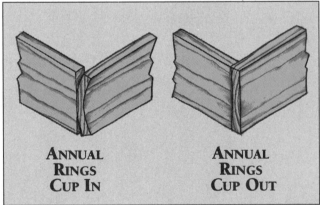

ANNUAL RINGS CUP IN   **ANNUAL RINGS CUP OUT**

2-3 When building boxes and chests, turn the boards so the annual rings cup *out*. There are two reasons for this, one practical and the other aesthetic. The practical reason is that plain-sawn boards have a tendency to cup in the direction opposite their rings as they dry out. If the rings cup in, gaps may develop at the corners. By turning them out, the corners will remain tight. Aesthetically, this arrangement displays more of the rich, colorful *heartwood* (the inside of the tree) on the outside of the box.

CORNER JOINTS

A variety of joints can be used to attach the rigid corners of a box, and the best choice depends on how the box will be used. Is it to be a strictly utilitarian storage unit, or must it be decorative as well? Will it see light duty, or will it be subjected to heavy use? Will it remain stationary, or be moved from place to place? Here are some of the most common corner joints (SEE FIGURE 2-4):

■ *Butt joints,* reinforced with screws or glue blocks, work well for light-duty, utilitarian boxes.

■ *Rabbets* and *dadoes* look the same as butt joints when assembled, but they are strong enough for medium-duty, utilitarian boxes.

■ *Miter joints* are more aesthetic — they hide the end grain on the adjoining boards so all you see is uninterrupted face grain. However, they are comparatively weak and best suited for light-duty projects. (SEE FIGURES 2-5 AND 2-6.)

■ *Splined miters* are much stronger than ordinary miters and can be used for medium-duty or even heavy-duty decorative boxes. The splines can be hidden or openly visible. SEE FIGURE 2-7 or refer to "Making Decorative Open-Spline Miters" on page 30 for more information.

■ *Finger joints* (once known as *box joints*) are strong enough to qualify for heavy-duty boxes and chests. The interlocking tenons create a vast gluing surface which holds firmly. They were once considered strictly utilitarian — many packing crates in the late nineteenth and early twentieth centuries were made with finger joints. In recent years, they have been used in decorative applications as well. (*SEE FIGURE 2-8.*)

■ *Through dovetail joints,* the strongest of all common joints for boxes, are suitable for heavy-duty projects. Like finger joints, they were once thought of as utilitarian. Today, however, they're used for both utilitarian and decorative pieces. (*SEE FIGURE 2-9.*)

Note: Some craftsmen use contrasting colors of wood when making dovetails and finger joints so the joinery will stand out.

TRY THIS TRICK

When gluing the corners of boxes together, protect the *inside* surfaces with masking tape. If glue squeezes out of the joint when you clamp the parts together, the tape will keep the excess glue from sticking to the wood. To remove the squeeze-out, simply peel off the tape after the glue has dried.

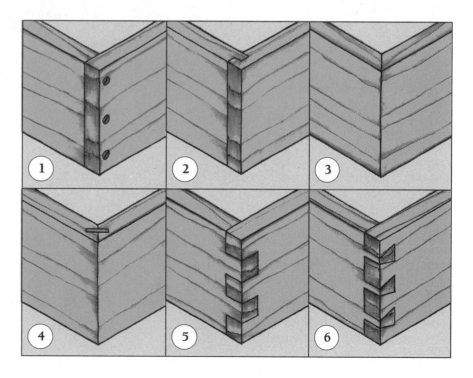

2-4 There are many joints that you might use to join the rigid corners of a box, but these six are the most common choices: a *reinforced butt joint* (1), a *rabbet-and-dado joint* (2), a *miter joint* (3), a *splined miter* (4), a *finger joint* (5), and a *through dovetail joint* (6).

2-5 For mitered corners to be as strong as possible, they must fit precisely, with no gaps. To test the angle of your table saw blade before you cut good stock, miter the ends of two scraps. Put these together in a square, pressing the outside faces of the boards against the inside surfaces of the square. If the miter joint gaps on the outside, the blade angle is less than 45 degrees. If it gaps on the inside, the angle is more than 45 degrees.

2-6 Before you glue the mitered corners of a box together, test fit the joints, holding the corners together with masking tape. When you're satisfied that all the corners fit properly, remove the tape from just *one* corner, but leave the others taped together. "Unroll" the box parts, using the tape like hinges. Apply glue to the miters, and reassemble the box — the tape will keep all the parts in the proper order and alignment. Don't remove the tape until after the glue dries.

2-7 To reinforce the mitered corners of a box with *hidden* splines, keep the blade tilted at 45 degrees after cutting the miters. Using the rip fence as a stop, make saw kerfs in the adjoining ends of the front, back, and sides, sawing the kerfs perpendicular to the mitered surfaces. If you make the splines from solid wood, cut them so the grain will run *across* the miter joint. (If you make them from plywood, grain direction is not a consideration.) Insert the splines in the saw kerfs as you glue the box together. **Note:** Make the kerfs as close as possible to the *inside* surfaces of the box parts. If they are too close to the outside, the kerfs will weaken the miter joints.

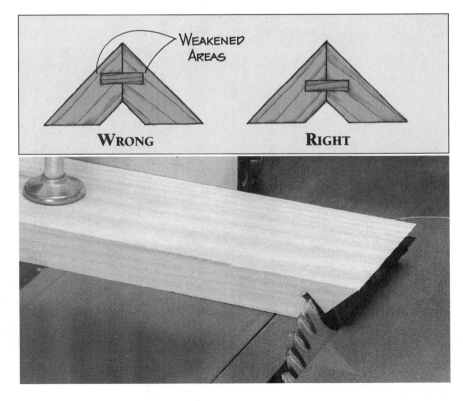

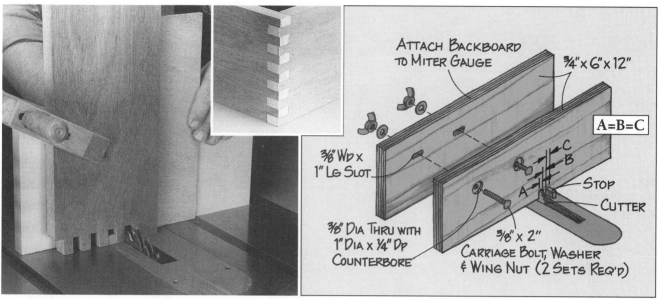

2-8 To make a finger joint, cut evenly spaced notches in the ends of the adjoining boards with a table-mounted router or a dado cutter. Attach a jig to your miter gauge to control the spacing of the notches — set up the jig so the width of the cutter, the width of the stop, and the distance between them are all equal. To cut the first notch, hold the board against the stop and pass it over the cutter. Place the notch you just cut over the stop and repeat. Continue until you have cut notches across the end of the board.

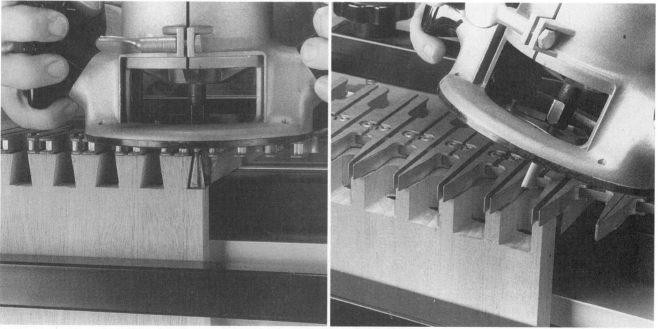

2-9 Of the many ways to make through dovetails, the easiest and most precise is to rout them, using a guide collar and a dovetail jig to guide the router. There are several commercial routing jigs designed to make through dovetails. The Leigh jig shown is available through most mail-order woodworking suppliers.

JOINING THE BOTTOM

Because the bottom must float, your choice of joints is more limited. On many boxes and chests, the bottom is captured in grooves. These grooves are cut in the inside surfaces of the front, back, and sides. (SEE FIGURES 2-10 AND 2-11.) You slide the bottom into the grooves at the same time you assemble the box, being careful not to get glue in the grooves. Once the glue dries, the bottom will be permanently installed.

If the project requires a removable bottom, or if you must install the bottom after the other parts are joined, rest the bottom on ledges or cleats. (SEE FIGURE 2-12.) Or, screw it to the bottom edges of the box, driving the screws through slots. (SEE FIGURES 2-13 AND 2-14.)

When fitting the bottom, remember to leave space for expansion. How much space? That depends on the width of the bottom. The rule of thumb is to allow ¼ inch for every 12 inches *across* the grain. See pages 36 and 37 for more information.

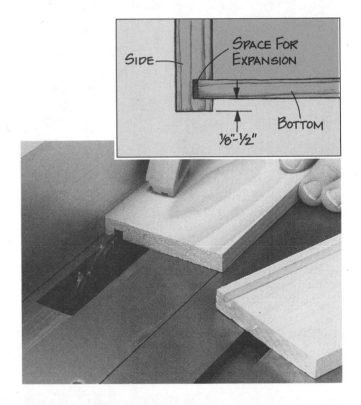

2-10 Cut the grooves for the bottom in the front, back, and sides with a table-mounted router, a dado cutter, or a table saw blade. The grooves should be close to the bottom edges of the box, but not too close or the bottom may be weak. For light-duty boxes, leave at least ⅛ inch of stock between the bottom edges and the grooves. For boxes that will see more wear and tear, leave ¼ to ½ inch.

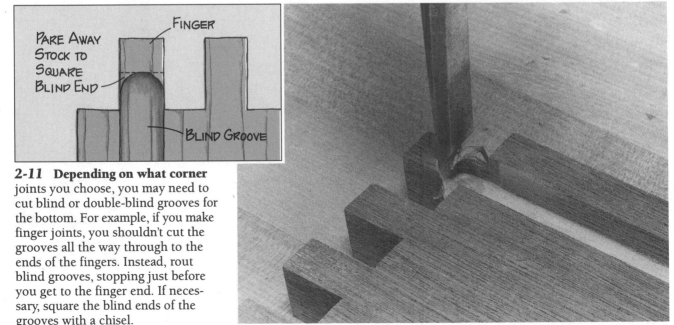

2-11 Depending on what corner joints you choose, you may need to cut blind or double-blind grooves for the bottom. For example, if you make finger joints, you shouldn't cut the grooves all the way through to the ends of the fingers. Instead, rout blind grooves, stopping just before you get to the finger end. If necessary, square the blind ends of the grooves with a chisel.

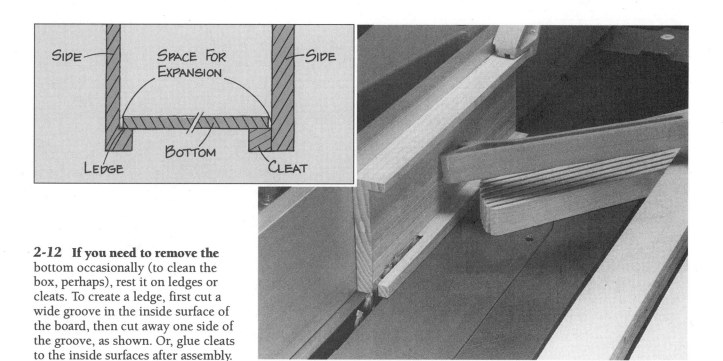

SIDE — SPACE FOR EXPANSION — SIDE

BOTTOM

LEDGE — CLEAT

2-12 If you need to remove the bottom occasionally (to clean the box, perhaps), rest it on ledges or cleats. To create a ledge, first cut a wide groove in the inside surface of the board, then cut away one side of the groove, as shown. Or, glue cleats to the inside surfaces after assembly.

2-13 You can attach the bottom to the box with roundhead screws and washers, provided you drive the screws through *slots* so the bottom can expand and contract. To make a slot in the bottom, first drill a large counterbore, deep enough to hold the head of the screw below the wood surface. Then drill a line of smaller holes through the bottom inside the counterbore. **Note:** The line of holes must be parallel to the direction of the wood movement.

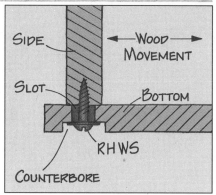

SIDE — WOOD MOVEMENT

SLOT — BOTTOM

RHWS

COUNTERBORE

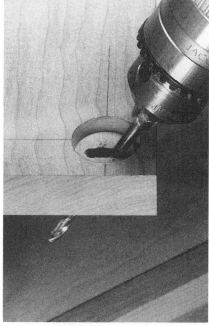

2-14 Create the slot by inserting the drill bit in one of the middle holes and angling it back and forth to remove the waste between the holes. When you drive screws through the slots, tighten them until the heads are snug, but not so tight that the washers begin to bite into the wood. If the screws are too tight, they will interfere with the wood movement.

MAKING DECORATIVE OPEN-SPLINE MITERS

Traditionally, splines are thin slices of wood or plywood, hidden inside a miter joint to strengthen it. However, when you make miters with open, *visible* splines, you can use different sizes, shapes, and colors of wood to decorate as well as reinforce the joint.

Unlike hidden splines, which are installed when the miters are assembled, open splines must be added *after* the joints are glued together. Assemble the box parts and let the glue dry thoroughly. Then mount the assembled box in the *Spline Miter Jig* — this fixture makes it possible to guide the box along a fence or a straightedge as you cut spline grooves in the corners. It can be used with either a table saw or a table-mounted router.

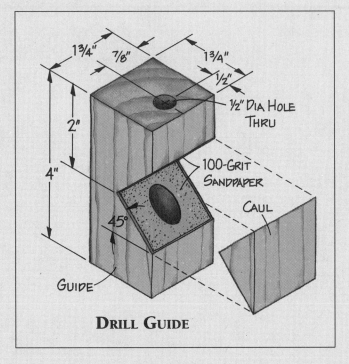

DRILL GUIDE

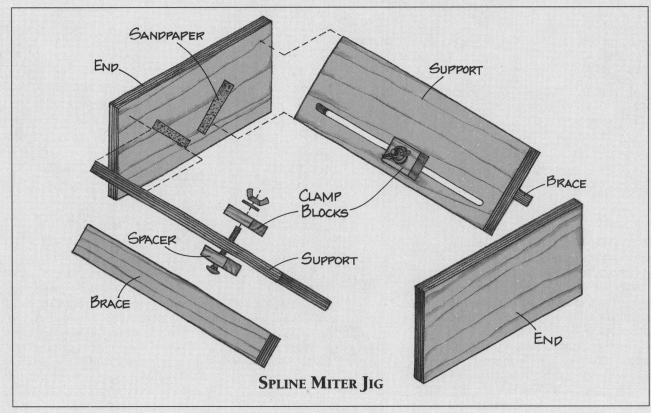

SPLINE MITER JIG

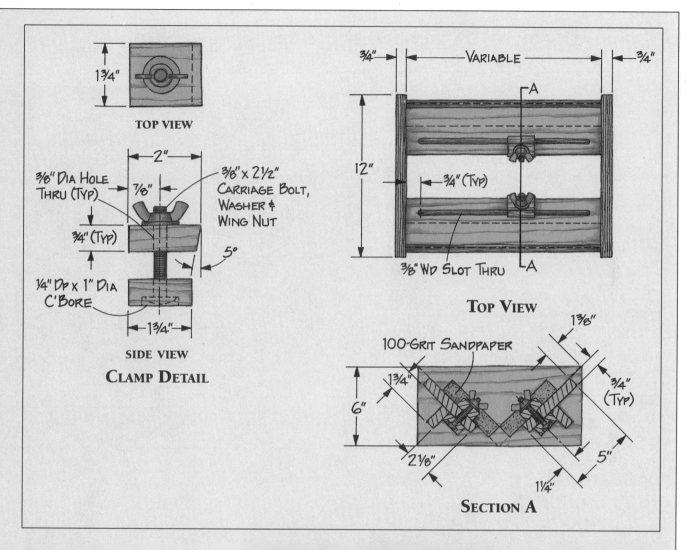

TOP VIEW

CLAMP DETAIL

3/8" DIA HOLE THRU (TYP)

2"

7/8"

3/8" x 2½" CARRIAGE BOLT, WASHER & WING NUT

3/4" (TYP)

5°

¼" DP x 1" DIA C'BORE

1¾"

SIDE VIEW

1¾"

3/4"   VARIABLE   3/4"

12"

3/4" (TYP)

3/8" WD SLOT THRU

TOP VIEW

A

A

100-GRIT SANDPAPER

1⅜"

1¾"

6"

3/4" (TYP)

2⅛"

5"

1¼"

SECTION A

1 **When using the spline miter** jig with a table saw, cut spline grooves across the corners of the box with a dado cutter or a flat-ground rip blade. (Flat-ground saw teeth leave a kerf with a flat bottom.) Adjust the fence to position the groove on the box. Make a cut in one corner, then rotate the box and cut another. Continue until you have cut all four corners. Move the fence to cut grooves in another position, and repeat. If you wish, tilt the blade or the cutter to saw the grooves at an angle. **Note:** Don't cut the grooves too deep; they must not go through to the inside of the box.

(continued) ▷

MAKING DECORATIVE OPEN-SPLINE MITERS — CONTINUED

2 **Cut splines to fill the** grooves. Make them from a wood that contrasts with the color of the box so they will stand out on the completed box. Glue them in the grooves, let the glue dry, and sand the splines flush with the wood surface. If you wish, you can repeat the process and add a second set of splines to the first to create more-intricate patterns.

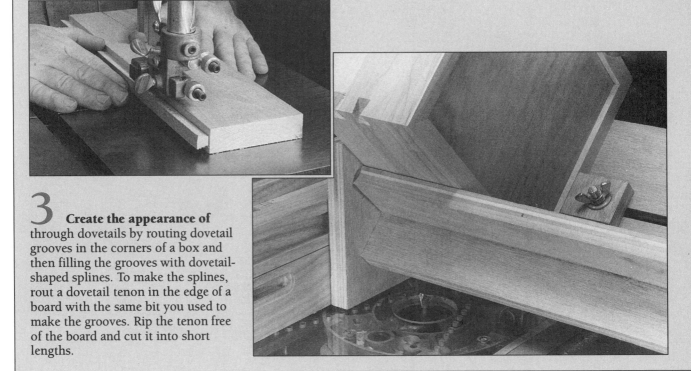

3 **Create the appearance of** through dovetails by routing dovetail grooves in the corners of a box and then filling the grooves with dovetail-shaped splines. To make the splines, rout a dovetail tenon in the edge of a board with the same bit you used to make the grooves. Rip the tenon free of the board and cut it into short lengths.

4 **Cut the dovetail splines into** short lengths and glue them in the grooves in the box corners. When the glue dries, cut and sand them flush with the surface. Once again, you can add a second set of splines to enhance the effect, if you wish.

5 **You can also use dowels as** splines. Make the *Drill Guide* on page 30 and clamp it to a box corner. Drill a hole through the corner at an angle to the box parts. Repeat, making several holes through each corner. Glue dowels in the corners, then sand them flush. Because the dowels are cut and sanded at an angle, they will appear on the completed box as ovals.

INSTALLING THE LID

The last part of a six-board box or chest to be installed is usually the lid. Like the bottom, this part must be allowed to move. However, there are many more ways to attach a lid than there are a bottom. Most of these can be grouped into two broad categories — fitted lids and hinged lids.

FITTED LIDS

A fitted lid simply covers the box opening. Gravity, aided by a rabbet or some other joinery, keeps it in place. Here are several common arrangements (SEE FIGURE 2-15):

■ *Rabbeted lid* — Cut a single rabbet around the perimeter of the lid. This will create a plug that fits the box opening and keeps the lid from sliding off the box. *Alternative:* Attach cleats or battens to the underside of the lid to make the plug.

■ *Rabbeted box* — Cut a single rabbet around the inside surface of the box to hold the lid. *Alternative:* Attach cleats to the inside surfaces of the box to support the lid. (SEE FIGURE 2-16.)

■ *Double rabbet* — Cut rabbets in both the lid and the box. The rabbets fit together when the lid is in place.

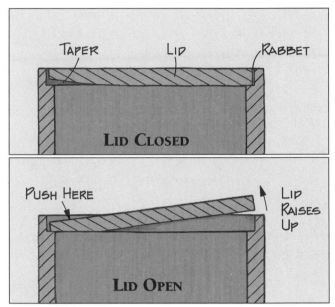

2-16   The fulcrum lid is an interesting variation on the fitted lid. The lid is supported on rabbets or cleats. It has no knob or fingerhold, and when closed, there appears to be no way to open it. However, the underside of the lid is gently tapered near one end. If you push on the right spot, the lid will lift up.

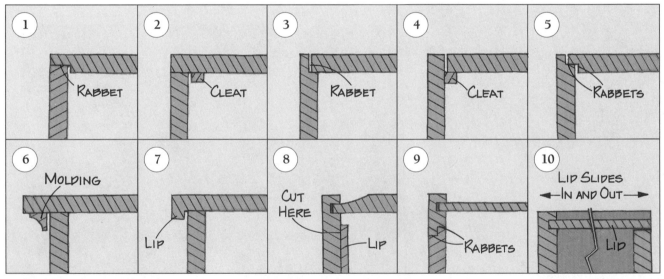

2-15   Shown are ten possible ways to fit a lid to a box. Rabbet the lid to fit the opening (1), or attach cleats to the underside (2) to keep it from sliding off the box. Rabbet the inside surfaces of the box (3) or attach cleats to them (4) to support the lid.

Rabbet both the lid and the box (5) to fit each other. Attach moldings to the underside of the lid (6) or rout out the underside (7) to create a lip around the lid. Cut the lid from the assembled box, then glue thin boards to the inside surfaces to make

a lip (8), or rabbet the cut-off lid and the box to fit together (9). Rout grooves in two or three sides of the box, cut the remaining side(s) short, then slide the lid in place in the grooves (10).

■ *Molded lip* — Attach molding around the circumference of the lid to create a lip. (*SEE FIGURE 2-17.*) *Alternative:* Rout a cavity in the underside of the lid and shape the edges.

■ *Cut-off lid* — Join the lid to the box in the same manner as the bottom; that is, cut grooves to hold the lid, and insert it in the grooves as you assemble the box. After the glue dries, rip the front, back, and sides to separate the lid from the box. (*SEE FIGURES 2-18*

AND 2-19.) Install a lip around the inside of the box to keep the lid in place. *Alternative:* Rabbet the outside of the box and the inside of the lid so they fit together.

■ *Sliding lid* — Cut grooves near the top edges of the front, back, and *one* side. Cut the other side short so you can slide the lid in and out of these grooves. (*SEE FIGURE 2-20.*) *Alternative:* Make grooves in the front and back, then cut both sides short — this will allow you to slide the lid in from either side.

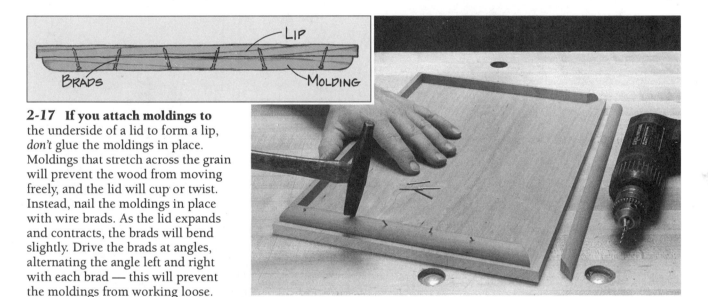

2-17 If you attach moldings to the underside of a lid to form a lip, *don't* glue the moldings in place. Moldings that stretch across the grain will prevent the wood from moving freely, and the lid will cup or twist. Instead, nail the moldings in place with wire brads. As the lid expands and contracts, the brads will bend slightly. Drive the brads at angles, alternating the angle left and right with each brad — this will prevent the moldings from working loose.

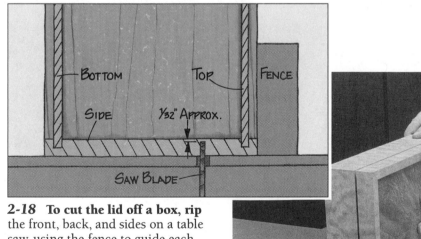

2-18 To cut the lid off a box, rip the front, back, and sides on a table saw, using the fence to guide each cut. Set the depth of cut so the saw blade doesn't quite slice all the way through the box parts. It should leave about 1/32 inch uncut. **Warning:** If you cut all the way through the wood on the table saw, the last cut may gouge the edges of the box or the lid.

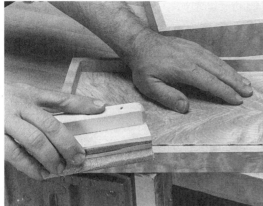

2-19 After ripping all four sides of the box, cut through the last $1/32$ inch of stock with a utility knife. Clean up the sawed edges of the box and the separated lid, removing the remaining tabs with a wood block and 100-grit sandpaper.

2-20 To make a sliding lid, rout grooves near the top edges of two or three of the parts — the front, back, and (possibly) one side. Cut the remaining parts short, so the top edges of the short parts are even with the bottom of the grooves in the taller parts. Cut or shape the lid to fit the grooves and slide it in place.

No matter what configuration you choose, remember that the lid must fit loosely, leaving room to expand. How loose should you make the lid? Plain-sawn wood expands and contracts up to $1/4$ inch *across* the grain for every 12 inches of width. Quarter-sawn wood moves approximately half that distance. (*SEE FIGURE 2-21.*) Although most lumber is plain-sawn, you can usually find a few pieces of quarter-sawn mixed in with the stack. If you make a 6-inch-wide box lid from this quarter-sawn stock, you can fit it with just a $1/16$-inch-wide gap — $1/32$ inch on each side. If you

make the same lid from plain-sawn wood, the gap should be $1/8$ inch wide.

The time of year and your geographical location also affect how a lid should be fitted. In most of North America, wood shrinks in the winter when the humidity drops, and swells in the summer when it rises again. Fit a box lid loose in the winter, tight in the summer. If your shop is in the southwestern United States, your weather is drier than the rest of the country's and wood doesn't move as much. South-western craftsmen can fit a lid *slightly* tighter than woodworkers elsewhere. By the same token, the South is more humid, and southern craftsmen must make lids slightly looser.

FOR YOUR INFORMATION

There is a prevailing myth that a finish seals the wood against moisture so well that the wood won't move. This is not true. A finish will slow the absorption and release of moisture, but it will not stop it. You cannot fit a lid tight during dry weather, coat it with finish, and expect that it won't expand when the climate turns humid.

Also consider the tendency of the wood to cup. As mentioned earlier in this chapter, a board will cup in the direction opposite its annual rings as it releases moisture, then flatten out again as it absorbs it. Consequently, a wide lid may become distorted for at least part of the year. If you make the lid from quarter-sawn lumber, you needn't worry — these boards are relatively stable and are less likely to cup. If you use plain-sawn wood, however, consider adding *breadboards* to the ends. (*SEE FIGURES 2-22.*) Breadboards are narrow strips of wood joined to the ends of a lid so their wood grain runs at right angles to the grain of the larger board. These brace the lid and help keep it flat.

2-21 In plain-sawn lumber, the annual rings run from edge to edge. The wood moves as much as ¼ inch across the grain for every 12 inches of width, depending on the species. Quarter-sawn wood, in which the annual rings run from face to face, is more stable. On the average, the wood moves just ⅛ inch for every 12 inches of width.

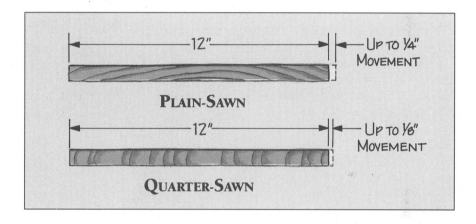

2-22 Join breadboards to a wide lid with tongues and grooves. Using a table saw or a router, cut long tongues in the ends of the lid, and deep grooves in the inside edges of the breadboards. To attach the breadboards to the lid, temporarily assemble the parts and drill holes through the tongue-and-groove joints. Disassemble the parts and enlarge the holes in the tongues to make slots perpendicular to the wood grain (and parallel to the direction the wood will move). Attach the breadboards to the lid by driving pegs though the holes and slots. Glue or pin the pegs in the breadboard holes (but *don't* glue them in the slots or glue the tongues in the grooves). This arrangement will allow the lid to expand and contract freely.

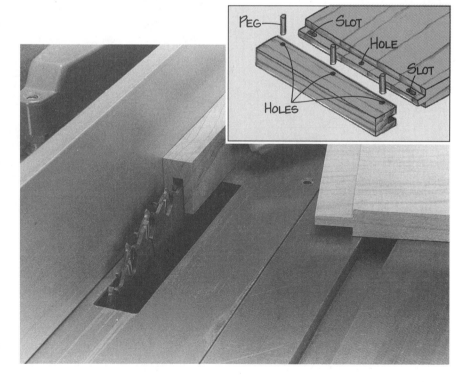

HINGED LIDS

There are hundreds of box hinges, each designed for a different purpose or aesthetic effect. (Refer to "Box Hardware" on page 41 for an illustrated list of the most common types.) These can be installed either on the surface of the wood or in mortises cut into the surface. (SEE FIGURES 2-23 AND 2-24.)

Surface-mounted hinges are the easiest to install. Temporarily wedge the lid in place or hold it to the box with double-faced carpet tape. Position the hinge on the wood surface and fasten it in place. (SEE FIGURE 2-25.) Mortised hinges require more work. You must measure and mark the position of the hinge on the box and the lid, cut or rout the mortises, then attach the hinge to the lid and the box. (SEE FIGURES 2-26 THROUGH 2-28.)

If you can't find a hinge for a particular box, consider pivots. Pivots are metal pins on which the lid rotates. Unlike hinges, which can be installed after a box is built, pivots are usually installed when you assemble the box. You must fit the lid before you glue up the box parts. (SEE FIGURE 2-29.)

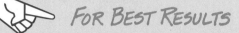

FOR BEST RESULTS

Use Vix bits to drill pilot holes when installing hinges and other hardware. These special drill bits automatically center the pilot holes so the heads of the screws seat properly in the hinge leaves. They are available through most mail-order woodworking suppliers.

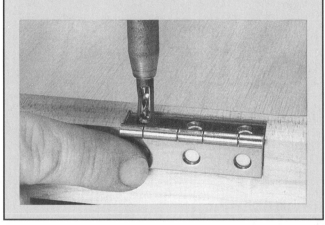

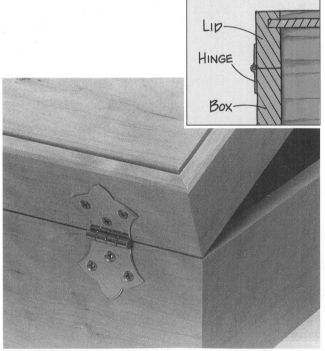

2-23 This butterfly hinge is a typical *surface-mounted* hinge. It requires no mortise or inset; it simply straddles the box and the lid. The knuckle is positioned over the joint between the two.

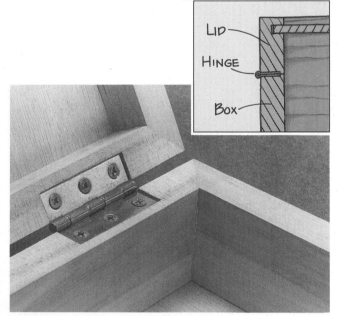

2-24 The common butt hinge is the most widely used *mortised* hinge. Each leaf is set in a shallow recess, or mortise, so the hinge is flush with the surrounding surface. One leaf is set in the edge of the box, the other in the edge of the lid. When the lid is closed, only the knuckle of the hinge is visible.

2-25 Although surface-mounted hinges are relatively easy to install, it can be difficult keeping the box, lid, and hinges properly positioned while you do so. To simplify this task, use double-faced carpet tape to hold the lid on the box *and* to hold the hinges in place while you drill screw holes. After making the holes, remove the hinges and discard the tape. Then fasten the hinges to the box and lid.

2-26 To set a butt hinge, temporarily assemble the lid and the box. If necessary, tape them together to prevent the parts from shifting. Draw lines across the joint between the lid and box, marking the positions of the hinges. Take the lid and the box apart and outline the hinge mortises on the adjoining edges. To outline a hinge mortise, stick one hinge leaf down with carpet tape and trace around it with the point of a knife or chisel. Remove the hinge and discard the tape.

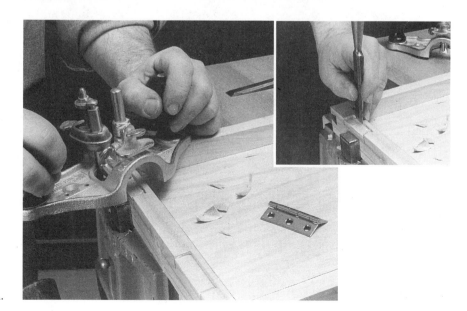

2-27 To make the mortise, first cut the sides with a chisel. Also use the chisel to clean out most of the waste, but don't cut the mortise to its final depth. Use a *router plane* to remove the last $1/32$ inch of waste. This simple hand tool cuts a flat-bottomed mortise to a uniform depth.

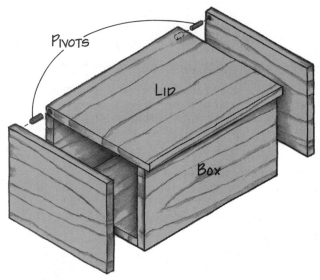

2-28 After making each mortise, temporarily place the hinge in it and drill screw holes. Fasten the hinges to the lid, then fasten the lid to the box. Test the lid action. If you need to shift a hinge after you've installed it, remove the screws and fill the screw holes with glue and toothpicks. Enlarge the mortise, if necessary, then drill new screw holes.

2-29 When there isn't room for a hinge, or you don't want hinges to show, use *pivots*. Drill stopped holes in the lid and the box where you want the lid to rotate. Assemble the box and lid *without* glue, inserting metal pins in the holes. Check the action of the lid. When you're satisfied it operates properly, glue the box together.

SECRET COMPARTMENTS

Create a secret compartment in the bottom of a box by installing a *false bottom* on cleats, just above the true bottom. Drill a small poke hole in the true bottom, near one edge. To remove the false bottom, poke a dowel or a pencil up through the true bottom.

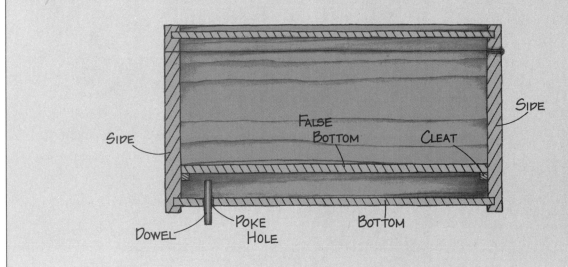

Box Hardware

SURFACE-MOUNTED HINGES

1. **BUTTERFLY HINGE** — Decorative; fasten to outside of box.

2. **H- AND L-HINGES** — Decorative; fasten to outside of box. Often used with framed lids or doors.

3. **NO-MORTISE HINGE** — Partially concealed; fasten to adjoining edges of box and lid.

4. **FLANGE HINGE** — Partially concealed; fasten to edge of box and inside surface of lid. Often used for blanket chests and toy boxes.

5. **PIANO HINGE** — Can be partially concealed or fastened to outside of box. Use when hinge must support much weight.

MORTISED HINGES

6. **BUTT HINGE** — Partially concealed; mortise adjoining edge of box and lid.

7. **CABINET HINGE** — Similar to butt hinges, but has decorative pin.

8. **KNIFE HINGE** — Almost completely concealed; mortise edges of lid and inside surfaces of box.

9. **LINK HINGE** — Completely concealed; mortise adjoining edges of box and lid.

10. **BARREL HINGE** — Completely concealed; bore holes in adjoining edges of box and lid.

LID SUPPORTS

11. **STRAIGHT SUPPORT** — Sliding support arm; fasten to inside surfaces of box and lid.

12. **CURVED SUPPORT** — Sliding support arm; use where space is limited.

13. **FOLDING SUPPORT** — Hinged support arm; use where space is limited.

14. **CONCEALED SUPPORT** — Sliding support arm; mortise adjoining edges of box and lid.

15. **TOY BOX LID SUPPORT** — Hinged support arm with tension spring; helps support heavy lids.

(continued) ▷

Box Hardware — continued

CATCHES

16. DRAW CATCH

Two interlocking plates held together with metal loop. Fasten to outside of box.

17. HINGED CATCH

Two plates held together with punched leaf and pin. Fasten to outside of box.

18. HOOK AND EYE

Hook pivots to catch eye screw. Fasten to outside of box.

19. BULLET CATCH

Spring-loaded ball catches in depression. Drill holes in adjoining surfaces of box and door.

20. BALL CATCH

Metal prong held by spring-loaded balls. Fasten to inside of box.

LOCKS

21. CHEST LOCK

Tongue in lock hooks strike plate. Mortise adjoining edges of box and lid.

22. CUPBOARD LOCK

Tongue in lock catches inside edge of box. Fasten to inside of lid or door.

23. PIN LOCK

Pin pushes into hole in box to prevent lid or door from moving. Often used for sliding doors.

24. CAM LOCK

Tongue pivots to catch inside edge of box. Drill hole in lid or door.

25. HASP AND PADLOCK

Leaf fits over wire loop; padlock prevents them from coming apart. Fasten to outside of box.

PULLS AND MISCELLANEOUS

26. KNOBS

Fasten to outside of lid for fingerhold.

27. RING PULLS

Fasten to outside of lid for fingerhold.

28. CHEST HANDLE

Fasten to outside of box to help carry.

29. CORNER PROTECTORS

Fasten to outside of box and lid to protect corners from damage.

30. FEET

Decorative; fasten to bottom of box to elevate box.

3

MAKING JOINED BOXES AND CHESTS

Medieval joyners found there was a practical limit to how large they could make six-board chests. Bigger chests required wider boards, and as boards grew wider, problems with expansion, contraction, and stability multiplied. However, by the beginning of the Renaissance, they licked these problems by borrowing a simple house-building technique: frame-and-panel joinery.

This method was originally developed to panel the interiors of stone and brick buildings. Moisture condensed on the masonry walls, causing wood paneling to expand and contract a great deal. So builders made frames of small, narrow boards in which larger panels could *float*. The movement of the smaller boards was negligible, and the larger boards could move without stressing the overall structure.

When used in furniture making, frame-and-panel joinery made it possible to build durable chests and large box-like *cases*. It became an invaluable component in *case construction* and is used today to build cupboards, cabinets, and other large storage pieces.

TRADITIONAL CASE CONSTRUCTION

A case is a piece of furniture built in the shape of a box to store something. The basic forms are the chest and the cupboard, but there are many other case pieces — bookcases, wardrobes, secretaries, and chests of drawers, to name just a few.

While a case may use frame-and-panel joinery, it doesn't have to be made entirely from frames and panels. More often than not, craftsmen mix solid boards with frame-and-panel surfaces when building a large storage piece. When do you use a solid board and when do you use a framed panel? There are three circumstances in which a framed panel is better than a wide board:

■ When you need *stability*. Doors and lids, for example, must remain square, flat, and dimensionally consistent. Extremely broad surfaces may expand and contract too much if built from solid wood. (*SEE FIGURE 3-1.*)

■ When you must build a broad surface from *poor lumber* or boards with internal stress. Cut the boards into small pieces, eliminating the stresses and the defects, then reassemble them into frames and panels. (*SEE FIGURES 3-2 AND 3-3.*)

■ When a frame and panel will *look better* than a simple board. You can shape the edges of frames and raise panels to create a wide range of decorative effects. (*SEE FIGURE 3-4.*)

3-2 It wouldn't be wise to glue up this pile of utility-grade maple into wide boards. The knots and other surface defects would detract from the appearance. Furthermore, checks in some boards hint that there are probably internal stresses in the lumber that might cause wide boards to split and warp. This sort of wood is best used for framed panels. As you cut up the lumber into smaller pieces, much of the internal stress is relieved. Trim away the knots and checks, then joint and plane the frame parts straight and true. The assembled panels will be perfectly flat and square, without any defects that may cause problems later.

3-1 The turn-of-the-century craftsmen who designed and built this old icebox knew that the moisture from melting ice would cause the wooden parts to expand and contract more than usual. Consequently, they made all four sides using frame-and-panel joinery. As a result, the storage piece remained solid and square.

Frames may be incorporated into a case so their surfaces are either vertical or horizontal. Vertical frames are ordinarily used on the outside of the case to make the front, back, and sides. Horizontal frames are more often found inside a case, tying the sides together or supporting drawers. (SEE FIGURE 3-5.) Some frames have *glazed* panels, with glass instead of wood; and others have no panels at all. (SEE FIGURE 3-6.)

3-3 Frame-and-panel joinery also lets you use highly figured wood that isn't structurally sound. Without a frame, this figured maple would have been a poor choice for the door of a small chest. Although the wood is beautiful, it moves in unpredictable ways and may hide internal defects that would weaken the door. But as a panel in a frame, the figured wood needn't support any weight, and it can move in any direction without pulling the frame out of shape.

3-4 You can create many different aesthetic effects with framed panels simply by routing or cutting different shapes in the edges of the panels, the inside edges of the frames, or both. Shown are four of the many possibilities.

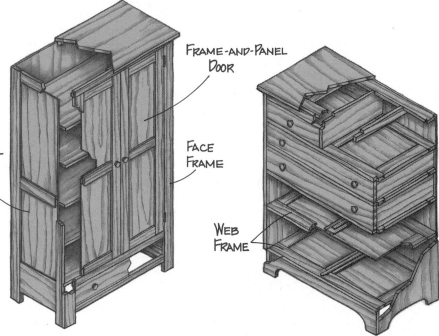

FRAME-AND-PANEL DOOR

FRAME-AND-PANEL SIDE

FACE FRAME

WEB FRAME

3-5 Framed panels can be used horizontally or vertically, on the inside or the outside of the project. The wardrobe shown has vertical frame-and-panel sides and doors on the outside of the piece. The chest of drawers has horizontal assemblies called *web frames* on the inside to support the drawers.

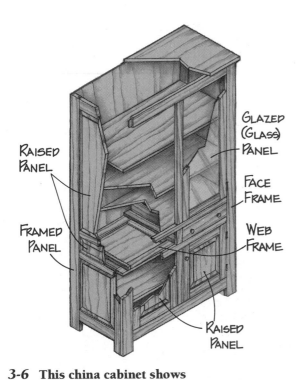

3-6 This china cabinet shows
several types of framed panels and
ways you might use them. The sides
and the bottom doors are vertical
frames with *raised panels*. The
drawers in the bottom section are
supported on a horizontal *web frame*.
The top doors are *glazed panels* —
frames with glass panes. Both the top
and bottom doors are mounted to a
face frame — a frame without any
panels, just openings for drawers
and doors.

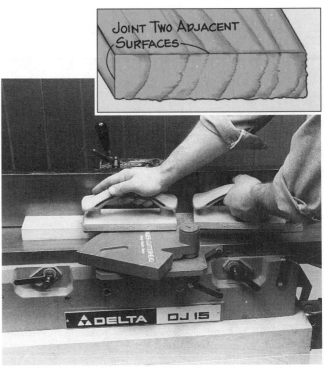

3-7 For the frame to be square
and flat, you must properly prepare
the wood to make the rails and
stiles. Choose clear, straight-grained
wood with no visible defects, then
cut the frame members to *rough* size
— slightly longer, wider, and thicker
than the final dimensions. This will
help relieve any internal stresses.
Joint one face of each member perfectly flat, then joint an edge square
to that face.

JOINING THE FRAME

Each frame has four *frame members*. The vertical members are *stiles,* which usually run the entire length of
the frame. The horizontal members are *rails,* which fit
between the stiles. The rails and stiles are joined to
make a rectangle. For the frame to be square and flat
(and remain that way) the members must be made
from straight-grained wood with no visible defects,
planed straight and true. (*See Figures 3-7 and 3-8.*)

To attach the rails to the stiles, use joinery that
resists *racking* — the forces that will pull the frame
out of square. Mortise-and-tenon joints are the
strongest for this application, and consequently they
are the traditional choice. However, you have other
choices. Here are five popular frame joints, all of which
incorporate grooves for the panels (*see Figure 3-9*):

■ In a *haunched mortise-and-tenon joint,* the tenon
is notched to create a small "haunch." This fills the end
of the groove in the stile. (*See Figures 3-10 through 3-13.*)

■ A *bridle joint* is a simplified form of a through
mortise and tenon — the mortise goes through the
stile, making the end of the tenon visible. Although
it's not quite as strong as a true mortise-and-tenon
joint, a bridle joint can be made with an ordinary
table saw and circular saw blade. (*See Figure 3-14.*)

■ In a *loose tenon joint,* both the end of the rail and
the edge of the stile are mortised. The two mortises
are joined with a spline or "loose tenon." (For more
information, see "Making Loose Tenon Joints" on
page 51.)

(continued on page 50)

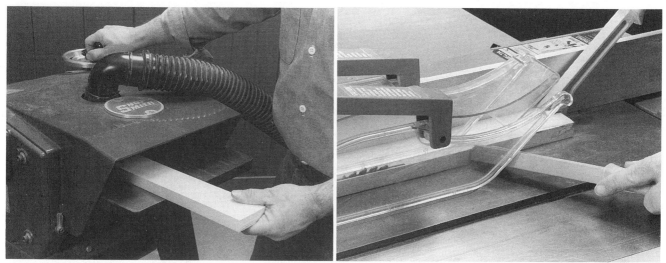

3-8 After jointing two adjacent surfaces straight and flat, plane the second face parallel to the first. Rip the board to its final width and cut it to length. **Note:** Some craftsmen prefer to rip a board to within 1/32 inch of its final width, then remove the last little bit of stock with a jointer.

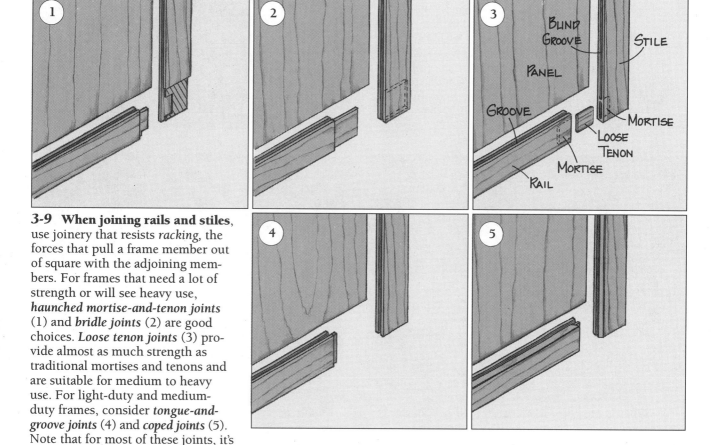

3-9 When joining rails and stiles, use joinery that resists *racking,* the forces that pull a frame member out of square with the adjoining members. For frames that need a lot of strength or will see heavy use, *haunched mortise-and-tenon joints* (1) and *bridle joints* (2) are good choices. *Loose tenon joints* (3) provide almost as much strength as traditional mortises and tenons and are suitable for medium to heavy use. For light-duty and medium-duty frames, consider *tongue-and-groove joints* (4) and *coped joints* (5). Note that for most of these joints, it's traditional to cut the tenon or tongue in the horizontal rail, and the mortise or groove in the vertical stile.

The exception to this rule is the loose tenon joint, in which both parts are mortised.

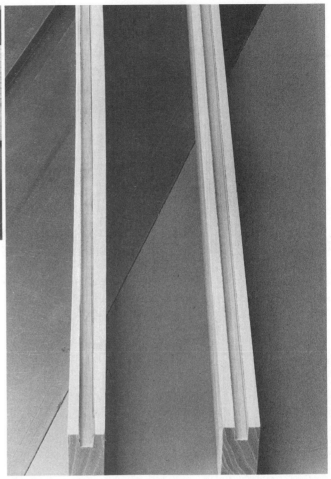

3-10   You can cut a groove in the inside edges of the rails and stiles with a dado cutter or a table-mounted router and a straight bit. One of the simplest methods, however, is to use a flat-ground rip blade on your table saw. With the rip fence guiding the stock, cut a kerf to make one side of the groove. Turn the board end for end and cut the other side. Besides being easy, this method also shows you when a board isn't straight enough to be used as a frame member. If the rail or stile is bowed or twisted, the sides of the groove will appear uneven.

3-11   When making mortise-and- tenon joints, most craftsmen find it easier to make the mortises first, then fit the tenons to them. It's easier to shave the cheeks of a tenon than the sides of a mortise. There are dozens of ways to make a mortise; shown is one of the easiest. Rough it out on the drill press, boring a line of overlapping holes. Then clean up the sides and ends with a mortising chisel.

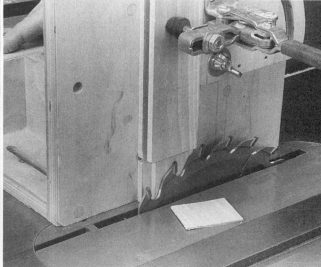

3-12 Again, there are dozens of ways to make a tenon or a tongue. Shown is just one possibility. Cut the shoulders, using the miter gauge to guide the board and the rip fence to gauge the length of the tenon or tongue. Then make the cheeks, using a tenoning jig to hold the stock vertical.

3-13 When making a haunched mortise-and-tenon joint, cut notches in the outside edges of the tenons to create the haunches. These haunches will fill the grooves at the ends of the stiles.

3-14 Bridle joints require a *slot mortise* — a deep groove on the end of the stile that fits over the tenon. Make these with a saw blade, using a tenoning jig to hold the stock upright. Cut one side of the mortise, turn the board face for face in the jig, and cut the other side.

■ A *tongue-and-groove joint* is adequate for most light-duty and medium-duty frames, provided the tongue is long enough and the groove is deep enough to provide a good glue bond. (*SEE FIGURE 3-15.*)

■ A *coped joint* is a decorative tongue-and-groove joint. The inside edges of the frame members are shaped as well as grooved. The ends of the rails are *coped* — cut in a mirror image of the shaped edge so they fit tight against the stiles. This shaping and coping requires a special set of matched shaper cutters or router bits. (*SEE FIGURE 3-16.*)

Remember that the grain directions of the rail and stile are opposed to one another. Because of this, the wood movement may stress the joinery if the parts are too wide. The rule of thumb is to keep tenons or tongues less than 3 inches wide and 3 inches long. If they are fairly narrow and short, the wood won't expand and contract enough to weaken the joint.

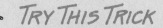

TRY THIS TRICK

For extra strength and durability, reinforce tongue-and-groove joints or coped joints with loose tenons. Rout matching mortises in the ends of the rails and edges of the stiles, *then* make the tongue-and-groove or coped joinery. When assembling the joints, insert loose tenons in the mortises.

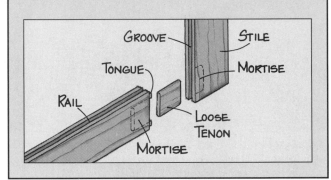

3-15 For a tongue-and-groove joint to be strong enough to withstand racking, the tongue and the groove must provide sufficient gluing surface. Cut the grooves at least ½ inch deep and the tongue ½ inch long to create this surface. You can increase the strength of the joint further by pinning the tongue in the groove with wire brads. Drive the brads from the inside surface of the stile so they won't be seen on the outside of the frame.

3-16 To make a coped joint, you must use a matched set of cutters for your shaper or table-mounted router. One cutter shapes the inside edges and plows a groove in them. The other creates the tongues in the ends of the rails, while *coping* the shoulders to fit over the shaped edges. In the completed joint, the shaped edges and the coped shoulders are mirror images of one another.

MAKING LOOSE TENON JOINTS

A loose tenon joint is best made with a plunge router. Rout two matching mortises, one in the end of the rail and the other in the edge of the stile. Join the parts by gluing a large spline or "tenon" in the mortises.

For the joint to fit properly, you must cut both mortises exactly the same size and position them properly on the adjoining boards. To help do this, make the *Loose Tenon Jig* shown. This jig guides the router and holds the stock as you work. The template attached to the fixed side is *reversible.*

There are two slots, each a different length, in the template. This allows you to rout two sizes of mortises — just flip the template face for face to change sizes. Make additional templates for more sizes.

The position of the template adjusts to center the mortise in the stock, and there is a stop on the fixed side to position the mortise along the length or width of the stock. Once the jig is adjusted, you can cut matching mortises in both the rails and stiles without having to change the setup.

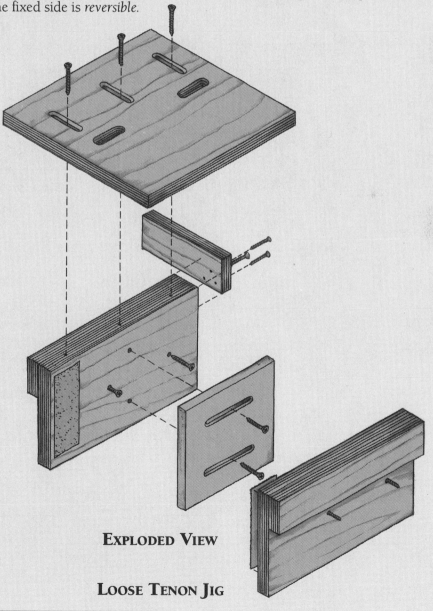

EXPLODED VIEW

LOOSE TENON JIG

(continued) ▷

MAKING LOOSE TENON JOINTS — CONTINUED

NOTE: Cut two router slots and countersink screw slots on both faces to make template reversible.

3/4"   3/4"

#14 x 1½"
FHWS
(2 REQ'D)   2"

SIDE VIEW

10"

1¾"
1⅜"
1⅞"

5/8" WD
SLOT
(TYP)

1½"

3½"   VARIABLE   #14 x 1½"
FHWS
(3 REQ'D)

10"

3½"

1½"   VARIABLE

1¼"

¼" WD x 2" LG
SLOT THRU WITH
C'SINK (TYP)

TOP VIEW

100-GRIT
SANDPAPER

10"

3"   6"

4"   4"

FRONT VIEW

MOVABLE FACE

¾"
5⅜"

2"

2"

¾"

#14 x 1½"
FHWS
(2 REQ'D)

½"

¾"

SIDE VIEW

FIXED FACE

100-GRIT
SANDPAPER

¼" WD SLOT THRU
WITH C'SINK (TYP)

5⅜"

1½"

#14 x 1¼"
FHWS
(2 REQ'D)

3"   6"

1½"

1½"   3"   1½"

6"

FRONT VIEW

LOOSE TENON JIG

1 **To use the jig, screw the** sides to the wooden faces of a bench vise. Make two adjustments — adjust the stop to position the mortise along the length of the stiles or the width of the rails, and adjust the template so the mortise will be centered in the stock. To mount a workpiece, insert it between the sides, butt the edge or the end against the workpiece stop, and tighten the vise. The jig will hold the workpiece either vertically or horizontally.

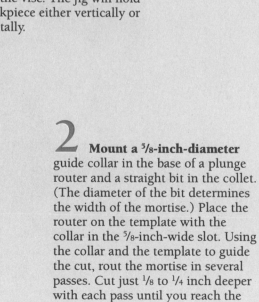

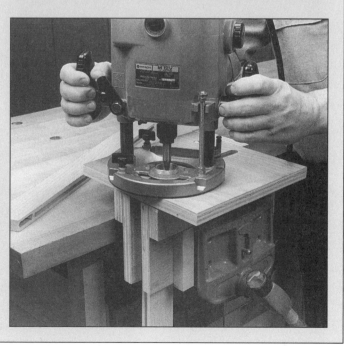

2 **Mount a 5/8-inch-diameter** guide collar in the base of a plunge router and a straight bit in the collet. (The diameter of the bit determines the width of the mortise.) Place the router on the template with the collar in the 5/8-inch-wide slot. Using the collar and the template to guide the cut, rout the mortise in several passes. Cut just 1/8 to 1/4 inch deeper with each pass until you reach the depth you want.

(continued) ▷

MAKING LOOSE TENON JOINTS — CONTINUED

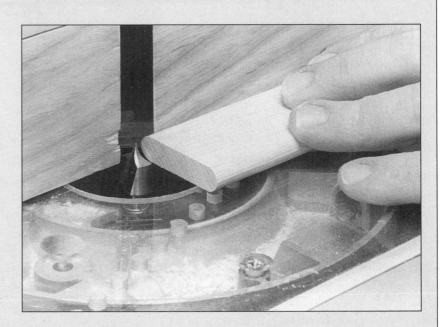

3 **Rip the tenon stock on a** table saw, cutting the thickness and width to match the width and length of the mortises. Round over the edges of the stock on a table-mounted router, using a roundover bit that matches the radius of the bit you used to rout the mortises. Then cut the tenons to length. Each tenon should be twice as long as the mortises are deep, minus 1/16 inch to allow for glue.

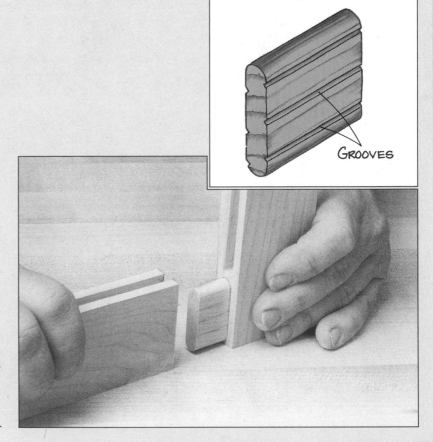

GROOVES

4 **To assemble a loose tenon** joint, make a few deep scratches along the length of the tenon with a knife or awl. (These scratches will relieve the hydraulic pressure of the glue when you press the tenon in the mortises.) Coat the sides of the mortises and the surfaces of the tenon with glue. Insert the tenon into the mortises and clamp the parts together.

RAISING AND FITTING THE PANELS

When you cut a panel to fit a frame, consider the movement of the wood. Remember, the wood expands and contracts up to ¼ inch across the grain for every 12 inches of width. During the driest part of the year (winter, in most locations), a 12-inch-wide panel should be ¼ inch narrower than the space allowed for it in the frame. If it's too wide, it may split out the edges of the frame or pop the joints when it expands.

If the panel is too narrow, it may shrink to reveal gaps between it and the frame, allowing you to see through the framed panel. To avoid this, cut the grooves that hold the panel deeper than the anticipated movement. For example, if you expect a panel to shrink and swell a maximum of ¼ inch, cut the grooves that hold it ⅜ inch deep.

The edges of the panel must fit the grooves in the frame. You can use a panel that's only as thick as the grooves are wide, or you can *raise* a thick panel to fit narrow grooves. To raise a panel, cut or shape the perimeter of the panel so the edges slope up to a raised middle. (The raised middle of a panel is known as the *field.*) The edges become thin enough to fit the grooves, but the field remains thick.

You can create different decorative effects depending on how you raise the panel. You might simply bevel the edges on a table saw, or you could cut shapes in the edges, using a router or a shaper. (*SEE FIGURES 3-17 THROUGH 3-20.*)

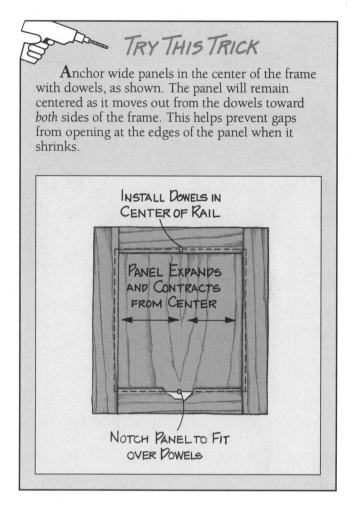

TRY THIS TRICK

Anchor wide panels in the center of the frame with dowels, as shown. The panel will remain centered as it moves out from the dowels toward *both* sides of the frame. This helps prevent gaps from opening at the edges of the panel when it shrinks.

INSTALL DOWELS IN CENTER OF RAIL

PANEL EXPANDS AND CONTRACTS FROM CENTER

NOTCH PANEL TO FIT OVER DOWELS

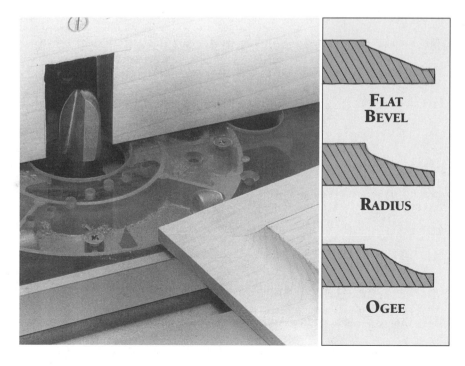

3-17 You can raise panels on a shaper or table-mounted router, cutting various designs in the edges. Shown are the three most common shapes — *flat bevel, radius,* and *ogee.* **Note:** When using a table-mounted router, choose *vertical* panel-raising bits to perform this operation, as shown. Traditional horizontal bits (called *wing* cutters) require more power and you must slow the router speed to use them safely. (At full speed — above 20,000 rpm — the tips of the wings move much too fast. A kickback could cause a great deal of damage.) Vertical panel-raising bits are safer, can be run at both high and low speeds, and require less power.

FLAT BEVEL

RADIUS

OGEE

3-18 To raise a panel on a table
saw, bevel the edges. Cut the ends of
the panel first, then the edges. If
there's any tear-out when you cut
across the wood grain, it will be
removed when you cut parallel to
the grain. **Note:** For safety, place the
fence so the blade tilts *away* from it
when raising panels.

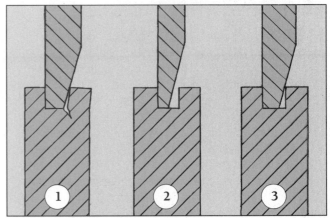

3-19 When making a raised
panel on a table saw, the thickness of
the stock where the bevel meets the
groove side is critical. If it's too thick
(1), the panel could split the frame
as it expands. If it's too thin (2), the
panel will be too loose and it will
rattle in the frame. The panel should
be snug, but not too tight (3): The
bevel should just touch the side of
the groove when the edge of the panel
rests in the bottom of the groove.

3-20 Raised panels often have a
step between the bevels and the field
to emphasize the design. Most router
and shaper cutters incorporate a step.
To cut steps on a table saw, carefully
position the rip fence so just the
outside corners of the saw teeth
break through the surface of the
wood as you cut. Afterwards, sand or
file the steps to make them square to
the field.

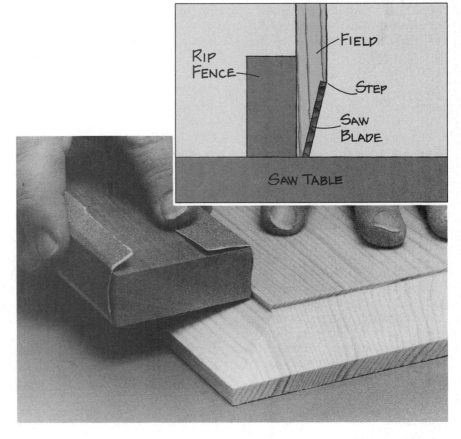

ASSEMBLING THE FRAMED PANELS

You can assemble a case from framed panels with many of the same joints you use to build a box from ordinary boards. Butt joints, rabbets, dadoes, grooves, miters, and splines all work well. (SEE FIGURE 3-21.)

However, you must use only the rails and stiles to join a framed panel to other assemblies. You cannot attach the edge of a board to a panel; it might restrict the panel's movement. In some cases, you may have to break up large panels into two or more sections, adding rails or stiles where you want to join other parts. (SEE FIGURE 3-22.)

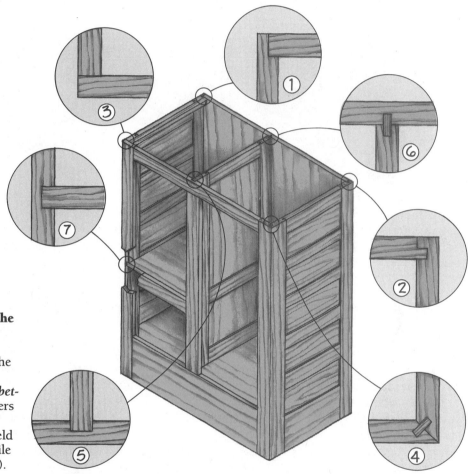

3-21 You can employ many of the same joints used in box joinery to assemble boards and panels. This hypothetical case shows some of the alternatives. The back corners are joined with a *rabbet* (1) and a *rabbet-and-dado joint* (2). The front corners show a simple *butt joint* (3) and a *splined miter* (4). The divider is held by a *groove* (5) and a *spline* (6), while the shelf is supported in a *dado* (7).

3-22 When attaching framed panels to boards or other framed panels, the parts must join the rails or the stiles. You cannot attach a board or a frame to a panel; the movement of the panels would be restricted. This filing cabinet case illustrates the problem. If you join the web frames to side frames with a single long panel, they will interfere with the wood movement. Instead, you must break the side panel into shorter segments, adding rails where you want to join the web frames.

RAIL

RIGHT   WRONG

ADDING LEGS TO THE CASE

Unlike a simple box, which rests on its bottom, a case usually stands upon feet, legs, or some sort of base. There are three simple ways to add a foundation to a case (SEE FIGURE 3-23):

■ Cut the outside vertical components of the case a little long and attach the bottom so it's slightly elevated.

Cut the shapes of legs or feet in the vertical parts.

■ Make L-shaped *bracket feet* and attach them to the bottom of the case.

■ Build a *base frame* and rest the case on it. If you wish, cut the shapes of legs or feet in the frame members.

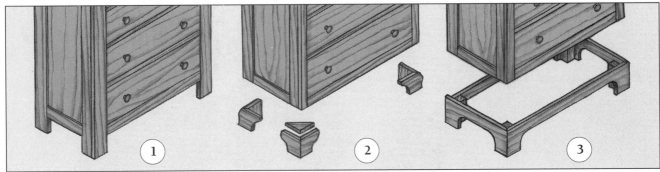

3-23 There are three simple ways to add a foundation to a case: Extend the stiles to make *legs* (1); build *bracket feet* (2) and attach them to the bottom of the case; or make a *base frame* (3) for the case to rest upon.

CONTEMPORARY CASE CONSTRUCTION

Frame-and-panel joinery isn't the only solution to the problems caused by wood movement. The invention of plywood in the nineteenth century gave craftsmen a viable alternative. This manufactured material is much more stable than solid wood, making it a good choice for large surfaces. Plywood also simplifies case construction, eliminating the need for complex joinery to accommodate wood movement. Building a large case from plywood is often no more complex than building a small box from solid wood. Today, it's used extensively in cabinetmaking and built-in storage units, as well as stand-alone furniture.

FURNITURE-GRADE PLYWOOD

There are many grades of plywood, each with a specific purpose. To choose the right material for a case, you should understand what's available to you.

Two types of plywood are commonly available — *hardwood* and *softwood*. Softwood plywood is used more often in building construction, while hardwood plywood is better suited for furniture making. However, some of the better grades of softwood plywood can be used in furniture as well.

Plywood is graded with a two-character code. Each character indicates the quality of one of the veneer faces. Hardwood plywood is graded with letters and numbers:

■ A is the "premium" grade; the veneers are carefully matched and joined.

■ 1 is the "good" grade; the veneers are not matched but there are no surface defects.

■ 2, the "sound" grade, may have small knots, discolorations, and other small defects.

■ 3 is the "utility" grade, with larger knots and some small splits.

■ 4 is the "backing" grade, with open knots and large splits.

Softwood plywood is graded with letters only:

■ N indicates a smooth veneer, cut from all heartwood or sapwood.

■ A is smooth with a few repairs.

■ B has tight knots, repair plugs, and small splits.

■ C has medium-size open knots and splits, as well as discoloration and sanding defects.

■ D has large, open knots and other defects.

When building a case with plywood, use A-2 (A on one side and 2 on the other) or better hardwood plywood for the visible parts. You can choose 1-2 or 1-3 for the inside parts that you won't see when the chest is closed. If you're working with softwood plywood, use N-B or A-B for the visible parts and no less than B-B for the others.

You must also remember that plywood is weaker than solid wood. It will not support as much weight without sagging, nor will it resist racking as well. Additionally, plywood doesn't hold nails and screws as firmly as solid wood, particularly when you drive those fasteners into an edge. (SEE FIGURES 3-24 AND 3-25.) However, all these limitations can be overcome with careful design.

3-24 When building with plywood, remember that although it is much more stable than solid wood, it is not as strong. It will not support as much weight as solid wood, as this demonstration shows. At the top, a 10-inch-wide plank of solid wood loaded with bricks sags less than 1/32 inch. At the bottom, a piece of plywood the same size and thickness is stacked with the same load. It sags noticeably. Try not to use plywood for horizontal components, particularly when these pieces must support a good deal of weight. If you must use plywood for a horizontal, load-bearing part, keep the span (the length of the component between vertical supports) less than 30 inches.

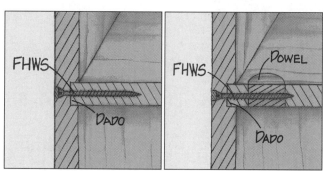

3-25 Plywood doesn't resist racking as well as solid wood; consequently, the joints between plywood parts may be weaker than the same joints made with solid wood. To compensate, many craftsmen reinforce glue joints with screws. But there is a problem with this practice, too — fasteners don't hold well in plywood edges. To solve this second problem, use 2-inch-long screws (rather than the usual 1¼-inch-long hardware). Or, install hardwood dowels in the plywood and drive the screws through the dowels.

JOINING PLYWOOD

There are two popular styles of plywood cases — with and without face frames. (SEE FIGURES 3-26 AND 3-27.) A face frame gives a plywood case a traditional look; without a face frame, it appears more modern. The presence or absence of a face frame also determines how the doors and drawers are positioned in a case. With a face frame, there are spaces between the doors and drawer fronts. Without a frame, these spaces diminish. The components usually butt up next to one another.

Stick to simple joints such as rabbets and dados when building a plywood case. (SEE FIGURE 3-28.) Complex joinery won't increase the strength of the case, and the material may splinter or chip if you cut intricate joints. If the project will see heavy use, or if there will be a lot of stress on the joinery, reinforce the joints with splines or glue blocks.

If you join plywood to solid wood, remember that the wood moves, but the plywood, for all practical purposes, does not. If the wood movement is restricted, the case may be pulled out of square, the solid wood

3-26 A *face frame* gives a plywood case a traditional look, spacing the doors and drawers apart. This solid wood frame is applied to the front edges of the case.

3-27 Without a face frame, there is no longer any space between doors and drawers; they butt up next to one another. This, in turn, gives the cabinet a more modern look. **Note:** Without a face frame, the front edges of the plywood case must be edged with solid wood or veneer to hide the plies.

3-28 A plywood case is just a big box assembled with simple joints. On the case shown, the vertical plywood parts — the sides and the back — are joined with *rabbets* (1), while the bottom rests in *dadoes* (2) in the side. The top butts against the top edges of the sides and back and is held in place with *cleats* (3). The face frame is attached to the sides with *grooves* and *splines* (4).

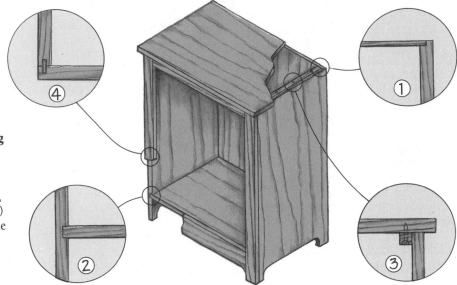

parts may split, and the joints may break. Depending on the width of the wood members and their grain direction, the project may require joinery that allows the wood to expand and contract.

How do you know when to accommodate the wood movement? The rule of thumb is similar to that which governs the width and length of tenons — if the solid wood is less than 3 inches across the grain, the movement will be small. You can join wood to the plywood without fear that the restricted motion will stress the case overmuch. However, you must allow wider boards to move, either by orienting the grain so the wood can expand and contract or by using floating joints. (SEE FIGURE 3-29.)

If any of the plywood edges are exposed on the completed case, you should cover them with veneer, laminate, or strips of wood to hide the plies. (SEE FIGURES 3-30 AND 3-31.) The reasons for this are both practical and aesthetic. Not only do exposed plies detract from the appearance of a project, the unprotected plywood veneers at the edges chip and splinter easily.

3-29 When joining plywood to wide, solid boards, consider wood movement. Either orient the wood grain so the expansion and contraction won't affect the structure, or use floating joints. Shown are three joints that allow a wood shelf to expand and contract against a plywood side. In the *dado joint* (1), the shelf is attached to the plywood only near the front edge. Most of the shelf is free to move in the dado. The screws that hold the shelf to the *cleat* (2)

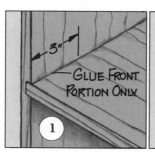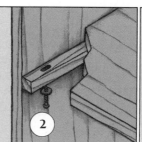

pass through slots. As the wood shrinks and swells, the screws move in the slots. In the *sliding dovetail*

joint (3), the shelf isn't glued or fastened at all. The dovetail keeps the parts together yet lets the shelf move.

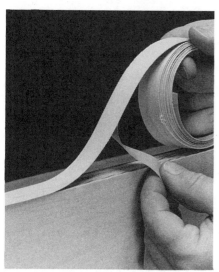

3-30 One of the easiest ways to disguise plywood edges is to cover them with veneer. Woodworking suppliers sell rolls of veneer just for this purpose. Apply the veneer with glue or contact cement, or use self-stick veneer tape (shown). After attaching the veneer, trim the edges flush to the plywood surface with a sharp chisel or knife.

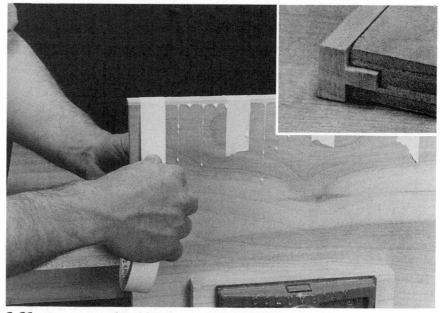

3-31 For a more durable edge, glue a ⅛- to ¼-inch-thick hardwood strip to the edge of the plywood, using masking tape to hold it in place until the glue dries. Afterwards, sand or scrape the edges of the strip flush with the plywood surface. Be careful not to remove so much stock that you cut through the plywood veneer. **Note:** If a plywood edge will see hard use, cut the hardwood strip in a T-shape. Rout a groove in the plywood and install the T-shaped strip in the groove.

4

MAKING CHESTS OF DRAWERS

The solution to one problem sometimes begets another. Case construction made it possible to build larger chests and boxes, but these eventually grew so big that it became difficult to reach the contents. Retrieving an item from the bottom of a large blanket chest meant moving most of the stuff on top.

Craftsmen dealt with this second problem in two ways. They built open-top boxes — trays — that sat within the chests. These trays made it easier to move aside one layer of stuff and get to the bottom of the chest. They also installed slide-out trays or *drawing boxes* in the bottoms of the chests, to permit reaching things on the bottom without

having to disturb the other contents. This last solution proved so popular that one-drawer chests (also known as *mule chests*) quickly gave way to two-drawer chests. Before too long, some savvy woodworker filled an entire chest with drawing boxes, creating what we call a chest of drawers.

MAKING DRAWERS

TYPES OF DRAWERS

A drawer is an open box (a box without a lid) that slides in and out of a larger box, chest, or case. Most drawers have five parts — a front, a back, two sides, and a bottom. Some have a sixth part, a false front or a drawer *face* that overlays the front. *(SEE FIGURE 4-1.)*

Drawers are classified according to how the drawer fronts and faces fit their openings. The fronts and faces may be *inset* within the opening; they can *overlay* the face frame or front edges of the case; or they may be rabbeted or *lipped,* and fitted so only the lips overlap the case. *(SEE FIGURE 4-2.)* The way in which the drawer fits its opening often affects the drawer construction and how it is hung.

DRAWER JOINERY

To a large degree, drawers are made like boxes. The front, back, and sides are arranged to expand and contract in the same direction and are rigidly joined at the corners. The bottom floats, free to move independently so its shrinking and swelling will not affect the drawer structure.

There are, however, important differences. Typically, a drawer must withstand more punishment than a box. As you push a drawer into a chest or pull it out, there is a good deal of stress on the corner joints. And because the drawer handles or pulls are attached to the drawer front, most of this stress is concentrated on the front corners. Consequently, drawers are com-

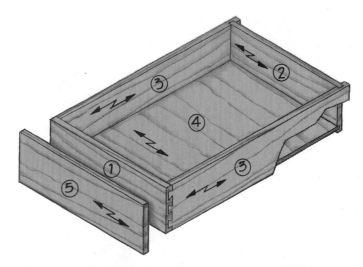

4-1 Drawers are open boxes that slide in and out of a larger box or case. Like a box, they have a *front* (1), a *back* (2), two *sides* (3), and a *bottom* (4). Some drawers also have a false front or *face* (5). As with other boxes, the front, back, and sides are rigidly joined at the corners, while the bottom floats so it can expand and contract independently of the other parts. However, drawer joinery is especially designed to withstand the stress of frequent pushing and pulling.

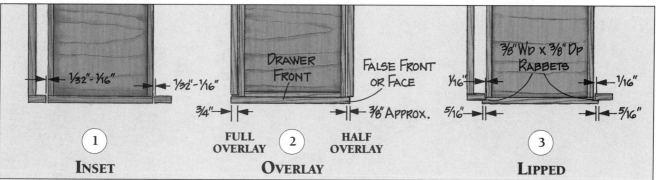

INSET — 1

OVERLAY — FULL OVERLAY 2 HALF OVERLAY

LIPPED — 3

4-2 A drawer front may be inset (1) in the case so the front surface is flush with the front edges or face frame. The front can also overlap or *overlay* (2) the case, partially covering the edges or frame. (Overlay drawers often have false fronts.) Or,

the drawer front may be *lipped* (3) — rabbeted all around the perimeter so only the shoulders of the rabbet fit inside the drawer opening. The lips created by the rabbet overlay the face frame or front edges.

monly built with extremely strong joints at the front corners, while the back corners and the bottom are assembled with much simpler joinery.

There is another reason for using different joints at the front of the drawer than at the back. In traditional furniture design, the drawer faces should look like solid boards or panels in a frame. Consequently, the

front joinery must be *hidden* when the drawer is closed. There are several joints that fulfill this requirement (*SEE FIGURE 4-3*):

■ *Reinforced rabbets* are sufficient for light-duty drawers. Rabbet the drawer front, then secure the sides in these rabbets with glue, nails, screws, or pegs. (*SEE FIGURE 4-4*.)

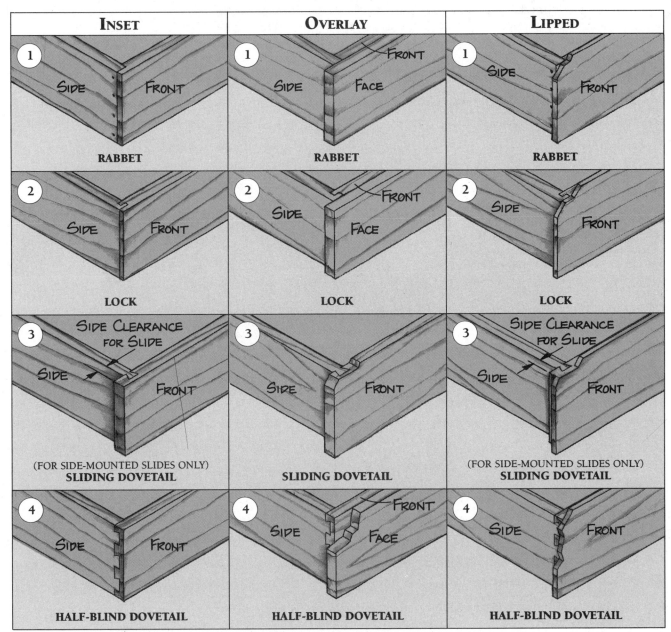

4-3 Four joints are commonly used to fasten the front corners of drawers: *reinforced rabbets* (1), *lock joints* (2), *sliding dovetails* (3), and *half-blind dovetails* (4). The way in which you cut and assemble these joints will depend on the type of drawer you're building — inset, overlay, or lipped.

■ *Lock joints,* also called tongue-and-dado joints, work well for light- and medium-duty drawers. Cut dadoes in the drawer sides, and tongues in the front. Insert the tongues in the dadoes. *(SEE FIGURES 4-5 AND 4-6.)*

4-4 Rabbeted corner joints are relatively weak because they have less gluing surface than more intricate joints. You can reinforce them with fasteners such as nails or screws, but small dowels or pegs will be stronger since these offer additional gluing surface.

4-5 To join the front and sides of a drawer with lock joints, first cut grooves in the ends of the front with a dado cutter or a table-mounted router. Position each groove off center, just ⅛ inch away from the back surface. Then cut the back sides of the grooves short to form ⅛-inch-thick tenons.

4-6 Using a flat-ground rip saw blade, cut ⅛-inch-wide dadoes in the inside surfaces of the sides. The distance between these dadoes and the ends of the sides must be equal to the width of the grooves you cut in the drawer front. To assemble the lock joints, insert the tongues on the ends of the drawer front in the dadoes in the sides. **Note:** For maximum strength, the dadoes must be as far from the front ends of the sides as possible. One way to do this is to make the tongues very thin, no wider than a saw kerf.

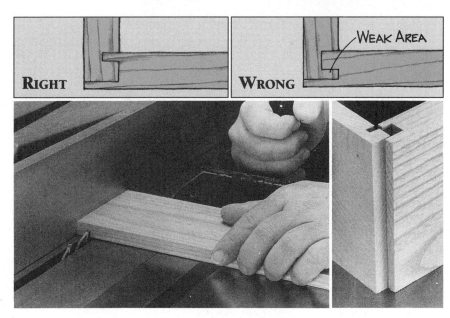

RIGHT   WRONG   WEAK AREA

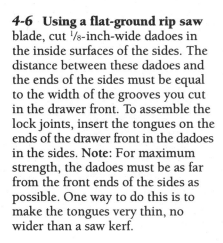

4-7 To make sliding dovetails, first cut dovetail slots in the inside face of the drawer front, using a table-mounted router and a dovetail bit. Cut tenons to fit the slots in the sides using the same bit and the same depth of cut.

■ *Sliding dovetails* are strong enough for medium- and heavy-duty drawers. Cut dovetail grooves in the drawer fronts, and matching tenons in the sides. Slide the tenons into the grooves. (*SEE FIGURES 4-7 AND 4-8.*)

■ *Half-blind dovetails* are the traditional choice when building heavy-duty drawers. The interlocking tails and pins offer enormous strength, and they are relatively easy to make with a router and a jig. (*SEE FIGURE 4-9.*)

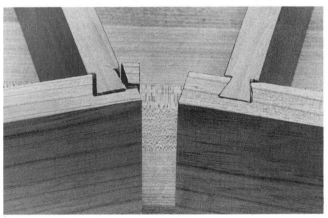

4-8 Sliding dovetail slots must not be too close to the ends of the drawer front, or the joints may split out. For this reason, sliding dovetails are best used for drawers in which the fronts protrude beyond the sides somewhat, such as overlay drawers or drawers that will be hung on side-mounted mechanical slides.

4-9 Commercial dovetail jigs enable you to rout half-blind dove-tails in one step. Clamp the adjoining parts in the jig end to face, so the boards form an L-shape. Secure the template over the corner of the L, where the parts butt together. Using a collar to guide the dovetail bit, rout both parts. The bit will cut the tails in the vertical board and match-ing pins in the horizontal board. **Note:** The slope of the tails should be 8 to 10 degrees in hardwoods and 11 to 14 degrees in softwoods, since soft-woods are more easily compressed than hardwoods.

In contemporary furniture, joinery is often used as a decorative element. When this is the case, you no longer have to hide the drawer joinery. Some contemporary craftsmen employ *through dovetails* and *finger joints* to join the front corners. (*See Figure 4-10.*) These are strong enough to withstand the stress, and they add visual interest to the drawer fronts.

You can use all of these joints on the back corners, but unless the drawer will see extremely heavy use, it's not necessary. Instead, use simple *dadoes, dado-and-rabbet joints,* or even *reinforced butt joints.* (*See Figure 4-11.*) These take less time to make than lock joints and dovetails but still provide adequate strength.

Extend the drawer sides 1/4 to 1/2 inch past the back, and let the sides serve as stops to keep the drawer from being pushed too far back in its case. (*See Figure 4-12.*) If you use dadoes or rabbet-and-dado joints, the extended sides will make the drawers stronger than if the ends were flush with the back.

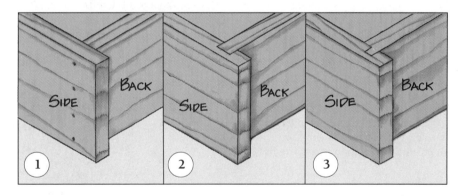

4-10 On some contemporary furniture, the drawer joinery becomes part of the decoration. For example, the drawers shown on the left have **through dovetails** (1), while those on the right have **finger joints** (2). Both joints appear as light and dark interlocking rectangles near the ends of the drawer fronts when the drawers are closed.

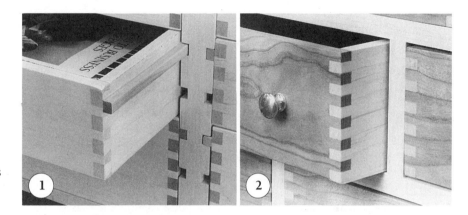

4-11 Because the stress on the back corners of a drawer is less than on the front, you can use simpler joinery. For light-duty drawers, use **butt joints** (1) reinforced with nails, screws, or dowels to join the back and sides. **Dadoes** (2) are much stronger and are suitable for medium- and heavy-duty drawers. **Rabbet-and-dado joints** (3) are stronger yet; use them for drawers that will see extremely heavy use.

4-12 To prevent inset drawers from being pushed too far into the case, let the back ends of the sides serve as stops. The sides make better stops than the back for two reasons. First, they are more stable. Should the back cup or warp, the drawer may protrude from the case slightly; should the sides cup, the position of the drawer won't be affected. Second, the sides are easy to adjust. Many craftsmen make them a little long, then cut or sand them to length when fitting the drawers. This way, they make sure the drawer fronts are perfectly positioned in the case.

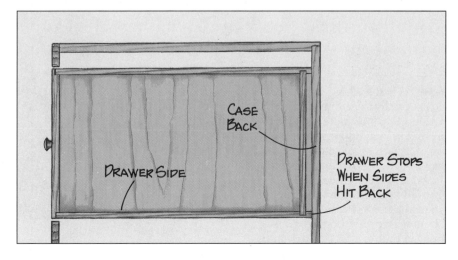

Drawer bottoms usually float in grooves. For traditional drawer construction, cut these grooves into the front and sides only. Make the back slightly shorter than the sides, and slide the bottom into its grooves *after* the drawer is assembled. Keep the bottom in place by driving a screw or a nail up through the drawer bottom and into the back. For modern drawers, make grooves in the front, sides, *and* back. Insert the drawer bottom in the grooves as the four corners of the drawer are glued together.

You can also cut grooves into small *slips,* then glue the slips to the inside surfaces of the drawer. A drawer bottom that rests in grooved slips is sometimes called a *French* bottom. *(SEE FIGURE 4-13.)* Finally, if the drawer is particularly wide — so wide that a thin bottom might sag — you can divide the bottom into two or more sections with grooved dividers or *muntins. (SEE FIGURE 4-14.)*

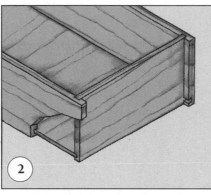
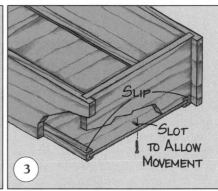

4-13 **A drawer bottom normally** floats in grooves so it can expand and contract without stressing the corner joints. There are three common ways to arrange these grooves. (1) When building a *traditional* drawer, cut grooves in just three parts — front and sides — and slide the bottom into the assembled drawer from the back. (2) For a *modern* drawer, cut grooves in the front, sides, and back, then insert the bot-

tom as you assemble the drawer. (3) To make a drawer with a *French bottom,* cut grooves in small *slips,* glue the slips inside the drawer sides, and slide the bottom in place.

Note: Traditional and French drawer bottoms are usually made from solid wood; modern drawer bottoms are made from plywood.

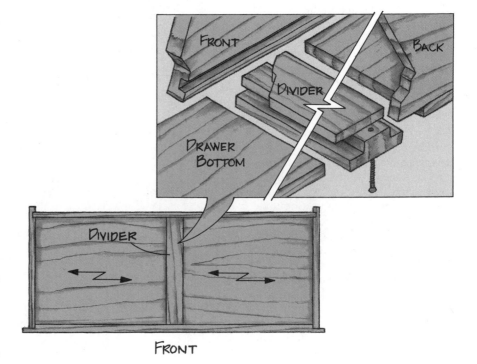

4-14 **When making an** exceptionally wide drawer, cut the bottom in two or more sections to prevent it from sagging. Join the sections with grooved dividers or *muntins,* as shown. **Note:** Sometimes the bottom faces of the muntins are grooved to follow drawer guides, as shown in *FIGURE 4-22.* The "Inspired Chest of Drawers" on page 86 uses grooved muntins and drawer guides.

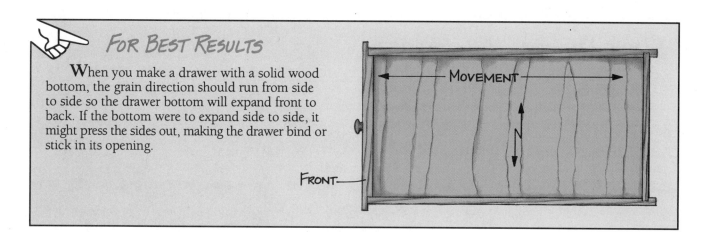

For Best Results

When you make a drawer with a solid wood bottom, the grain direction should run from side to side so the drawer bottom will expand front to back. If the bottom were to expand side to side, it might press the sides out, making the drawer bind or stick in its opening.

MOVEMENT

N

FRONT

SIZING DRAWERS

When determining the sizes of the drawers in a project, you must consider what you want to store in them. But that's just the beginning; there are several other important considerations. The drawer arrangement must be aesthetically pleasing, the joinery should be symmetrical, and there must be enough room inside the drawers to grasp the contents.

1 **When designing a project in** which the drawers are stacked vertically, such as a chest of drawers, place the deepest drawers on the bottom and the shallowest on top. If you put the deep drawers on top, the project will look top heavy. How deep should the drawers be? The rule of thumb is to make them in 1- and 2-inch increments. For example, you might build the deepest drawer in a chest of drawers 10 inches deep, followed by a drawer of 8 inches, then 6, decreasing in 2-inch steps. From 6 inches, let the drawers decrease in 1-inch steps — 6, 5, and 4 inches, respectively. **Note:** Unless you have a special need, don't make drawers deeper than 12 inches. It's difficult to retrieve stuff on the bottom of deep drawers.

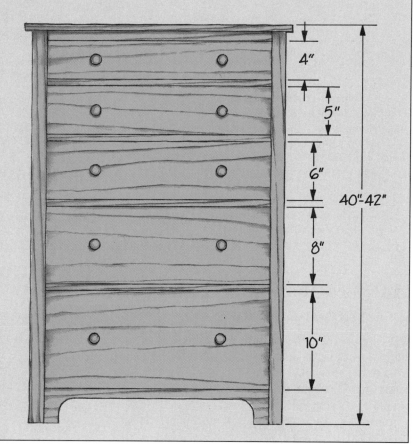

4"

5"

6"

40"-42"

8"

10"

(continued) ▷

SIZING DRAWERS — CONTINUED

2 **Also consider the joinery** when planning the depth of a drawer. If you join a drawer with finger joints, the depth should be a multiple of the thickness of the fingers — a split finger will look out of place. If you join the drawers with dovetails, the depth should be a multiple of the distance between the tails. Traditionally, craftsmen plan a dovetail joint with two split pins, one on the top and the other on the bottom, but the tails are left whole.

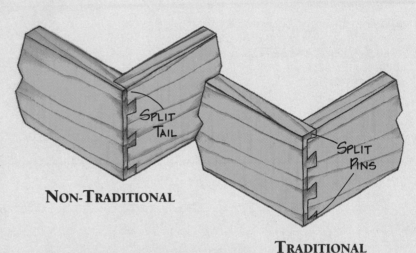

NON-TRADITIONAL

TRADITIONAL

3 **When making drawers or** compartments in drawers — especially small ones — remember to leave room for your fingers. If you make the drawer too small, or objects fit into it too closely, you won't be able to get your finger under them to grasp them. Remember, the basic purpose behind drawers is to allow you to retrieve things easily.

HANGING THE DRAWERS

SUSPENSION AND SUPPORT

You cannot simply set a drawer in a chest. You must *hang* it — make or install a framework for it to slide on. There are two basic ways to hang a drawer. You can either (1) suspend a drawer by its *sides* or (2) support it by its *bottom*.

You have a choice of three common methods for suspending a drawer from its sides (*SEE FIGURE 4-15*):

■ *Side-mounted guides* are narrow strips of wood that serve as runners to guide the drawers in and out of the case. Attach the supports inside the case and cut grooves in the drawer sides to fit over the supports. *Alternative:* Attach the supports to the drawer sides and cut grooves in the sides of the case. (*SEE FIGURE 4-16.*)

■ *Side-mounted slides* work like drawer supports.

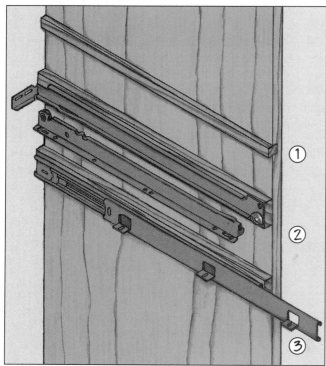

4-15 There are three ways to
suspend drawers from their sides.
(1) Attach *side-mounted guides* to
the inside of the case and cut grooves
in the drawer to fit them. (2) Install
side-mounted slides, attaching the
rollers and channels to the sides of
the drawer and case. (3) Attach *extension slides* to the drawer and case.

4-16 When you need the
maximum amount of drawer space,
use *side-mounted guides* to hang the
drawers. You can make wider, deeper
drawers with this arrangement than
with any other. Because the sides are
grooved to fit over the guides, you
don't need the great deal of side
clearance required for slide hardware. And since the drawers are
suspended from the sides, you don't
need to make room for frames or
brackets between them.

Each slide consists of two pieces of hardware — a
roller and a channel. One part attaches to the side of
the drawer; the other attaches inside the case. (*SEE
FIGURE 4-17.*) They must be positioned vertically to
hold the drawer at the proper height.

■ *Extension slides* allow you to pull the drawers all
the way out of the case without detaching them from
the supporting hardware. Fasten one end of each slide
to a drawer side and the other end inside the case.
(*SEE FIGURE 4-18.*)

For Your Information

When using side-mounted slides and extension
slides to hang drawers, build the drawers about 1
inch narrower than the openings. Each piece of hardware is about ½ inch thick, and you must allow some
side *clearance* for it. Extend the drawer face or front
past the sides to hide the hardware when the drawer
is closed.

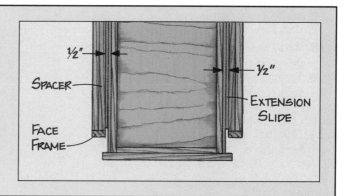

4-17 There are many types of roller-and-channel side-mounted slides, but they all work in a similar manner. The flanges of the channels ride the rollers, so the drawers actually roll in and out of the case. Each of the slides shown consists of two channels, and each channel has its own roller. One channel-and-roller assembly is attached to the drawer and the other to the inside of the case. When the drawer is installed, the rollers and channels interlock.

4-18 With side-mounted guides and slides, you cannot slide the drawer completely out of the case. You must leave several inches of the drawer inside it, or you'll dismount the drawer completely. Extension slides, however, allow you to pull the drawer almost clear of the case. This is handy if you often need to reach items that are stored in the rear of the drawer.

There are also several ways to support a drawer from the bottom (SEE FIGURE 4-19):

■ *Support brackets* are L-shaped wooden devices that cradle the drawers as they slide in and out of the case. Attach the guides inside the case. (SEE FIGURE 4-20.)

■ *Support shelves* are solid pieces of wood that span the distance between the two sides. They are no different than ordinary shelves except that they support drawers. (SEE FIGURE 4-21.)

■ *Web frames* are part of the case structure and support the drawers like shelves. Often there are cleats or guides near the sides or in the middle of the frames to help guide the drawers. (SEE FIGURE 4-22.)

4-19 Drawers can be supported from the bottom in any of four ways. Rest them on L-shaped *support brackets* (1) that are attached inside the case. Set the drawers on *support shelves* (2) or *web frames* (3). Install *bottom-mounted slides* (4), spanning the distance between the front and back of the case.

4-20   L-shaped support brackets
are perhaps the least expensive and
most versatile devices you can use to
hang a drawer. Each support is just
two pieces of hardwood screwed to
the inside of the case. They have
long been a favorite method for furniture makers to simplify the construction of large projects, but they
can also be used in small projects.

4-21   The drawers in this desk
box rest on simple support shelves.
As you slide the drawers in and out,
they are guided by the sides of the
box. This method is best reserved for
small projects; large shelves aren't
stable enough, and if they warp or
twist, the drawers will bind. Furthermore, large support shelves would
require too much material, adding
needless weight and expense to the
project.

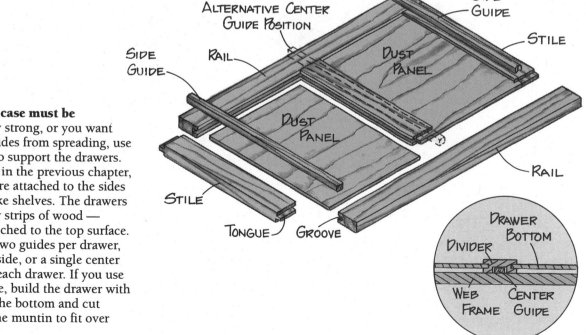

4-22   If the case must be
exceptionally strong, or you want
to keep the sides from spreading, use
web frames to support the drawers.
As explained in the previous chapter,
web frames are attached to the sides
of the case like shelves. The drawers
are guided by strips of wood —
guides — attached to the top surface.
You can use two guides per drawer,
one on each side, or a single center
guide under each drawer. If you use
a center guide, build the drawer with
a muntin in the bottom and cut
a groove in the muntin to fit over
the guide.

■ *Bottom-mounted slides,* like their side-mounted counterparts, have two components, rollers and channels. Attach the roller to the bottom of the drawer, and install the channel inside the case so it spans the distance between the front and the back. *(SEE FIGURE 4-23.)*

Note: Drawers mounted on drawer guides and web frames often need *kickers* — wooden rails above the drawer to keep them from tipping forward as you slide them out of the case. *(SEE FIGURE 4-24.)*

How do you know which method to use for a particular project? That depends on several practical considerations. If you need to save weight or simplify construction, you might choose side-mounted supports, extension slides, or drawer guides. These have few parts and are simple to install. To strengthen a case or keep it square, you may need to tie the sides together with support shelves or web frames. When money is an issue, consider simple all-wood supports such as support brackets and guides; they are less expensive to make than those requiring more material, such as web frames and shelves. Simple roller-and-channel slides cost much less than extension slides.

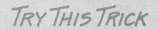

TRY THIS TRICK

To help drawers slide smoothly on wooden devices such as side-mounted guides, support brackets, and web frames, use nylon or Teflon tape to cover the surfaces where the drawers make contact. This reduces the friction between the wood surfaces.

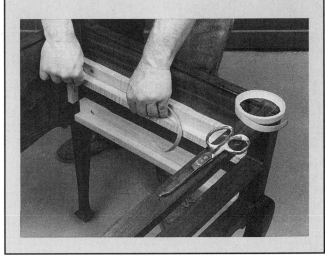

4-23 While most drawer-hanging devices attach to the sides of the case, bottom-mounted slides are fastened to the front and back. The case must have a face frame or front rails to attach the front end of the channel. Often there are rails at the back, too, to provide a sturdy anchor for the channel's back end. The roller is attached to the bottom of the drawer, near the back.

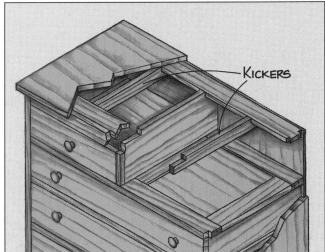

KICKERS

4-24 When hanging drawers on support brackets or web frames, you must make sure they don't tip forward as they slide out of the case. Where necessary, install strips of wood called *kickers* above the drawers to control tipping. In chests where the drawers are stacked vertically, the support or frame above each drawer may prevent tipping, so that only the top drawer requires a kicker.

FITTING THE DRAWERS

Size each drawer to fit its opening with a little play. The width of the sides and back must be slightly smaller than the drawer opening so the drawer will slide smoothly.

Additionally, you must take into account your geographical location and time of year when you fit the drawers. The same rule of thumb applies as when fitting box lids: Fit drawers loose in the winter when it's dry and the wood has shrunk, and tight in the summer when the wood swells with the humidity. If your shop is in the dry Southwest, where wood doesn't move as much as in the rest of the country, you can fit drawers *slightly* tighter than woodworkers elsewhere. If it's in the humid South, you must fit them slightly looser.

If you make many projects with drawers, you'll quickly find it's easier to fit drawers that are hung on *adjustable* devices than those hanging on fixed ones.

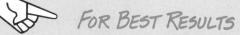

FOR BEST RESULTS

Build each drawer the *same size* as the drawer opening. It will be too big, of course. You'll have to plane or sand the surfaces, making it a little smaller than the opening for it to slide smoothly. However, if you try to build a drawer to its fitted size, there's a chance you will make it too small and the fit will be sloppy. It's easier to get a good fit if you build the drawer oversize, then sand or plane it to the proper size.

Often, you can stop a drawer from sticking or binding simply by moving a guide or support slightly. Many of the better drawer slides are adjustable, and you can make most of the wooden devices adjustable simply by cutting slots for the screws that you use to mount them. (*SEE FIGURE 4-25.*)

4-25 Drawers are much easier to fit when you use *adjustable* devices to hang them. Here are four that you can make. (1) Attach *side-mounted guides* with flathead machine screws and square nuts. Rout T-slots in the sides to fit the square nuts; this will allow you to move the guides up and down. (2) Cut counterbored screw slots in *support brackets* so you can move them up and down; use shims to move them in and out. (3) Cut slots and counterbores in web frames and attach center guides with machine screws and nuts. This will allow you to move the guides side to side. (4) Make eccentric drawer stops by cutting small wooden discs and drilling off-center pilot holes in them. To move the position of a stop, rotate the disc.

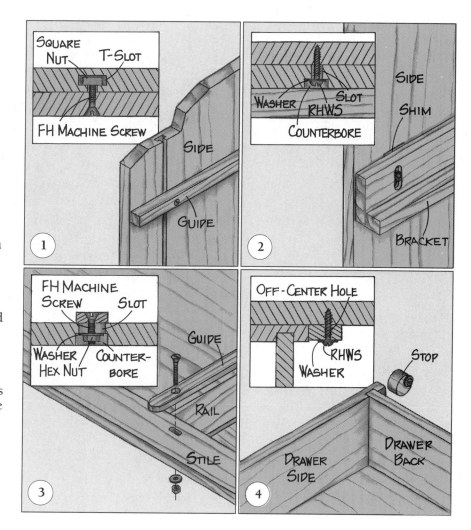

MAKING WOODEN DRAWER PULLS

In addition to hanging and fitting a drawer in its case, you must also provide a fingerhold to help pull the drawer out. There are thousands of commercial drawer pulls to choose from, available from hardware stores and mail-order suppliers. Or, you can make your own. Here are several methods you might use.

1 **Turn wooden pulls and knobs.** If you don't have a lathe, use a drill press. Make the *Drill Press Turning Jig* on page 78; install the drive center in the drill chuck and clamp the tailstock and tool rest to the worktable. Drill a $7/16$-inch-diameter, $1/2$-inch-deep hole in the top of the turning stock, and a countersink in the bottom. To mount the stock, place the countersink on the tailstock and press the drive center into the hole. Turn on the drill press and cut the shape of the pull with chisels. **Note:** If necessary, you can grind old chisels to the shapes you need. Otherwise, you can turn simple knobs with ordinary flat chisels, mortising chisels, and gouges.

2 **You can pattern rout a finger** pull with a hand-held router, using a template and a collar to guide the bit. There are special router bits available for this task, or you can use an ordinary dovetail bit, as shown. Start the cut with a straight bit and remove most of the stock from inside the pull. Then finish up with a dovetail bit, cutting the angle in the sides. **Note:** Choose a dovetail bit with cutting flutes at least $3/4$ inch long, or you may not cut deep enough to create a good purchase for your fingers.

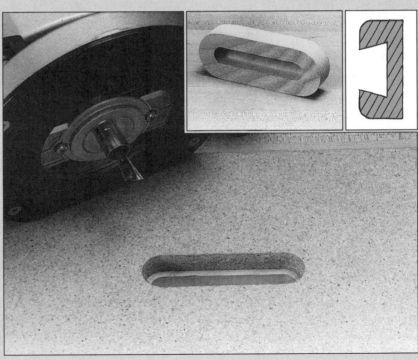

3 **Or, create a pull with a cove** bit on a table-mounted router. Rout a 3-inch-long double-blind cove in a length of wood, as shown. Cut the wood 4 to 6 inches long, centering the cove in the bottom back corner. Chamfer or round over the top front corner, opposite the cove.

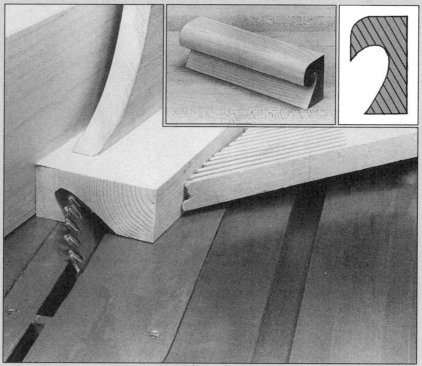

4 **You can also create pulls on** a table saw by making *angled* cove cuts. Tilt the saw blade at 45 degrees, and fasten a fence to the worktable at a 12-degree angle to the body of the blade. Adjust the depth of cut so just $1/16$ inch of the blade protrudes above the table. Turn on the saw and pass the wood across the blade, cutting a $1/16$-inch-deep angled cove. Raise the blade another $1/16$ inch and repeat. Continue until you have made the cove about $3/4$ inch deep, then saw the stock into 4-inch lengths.

(continued) ▷

Making Wooden Drawer Pulls — continued

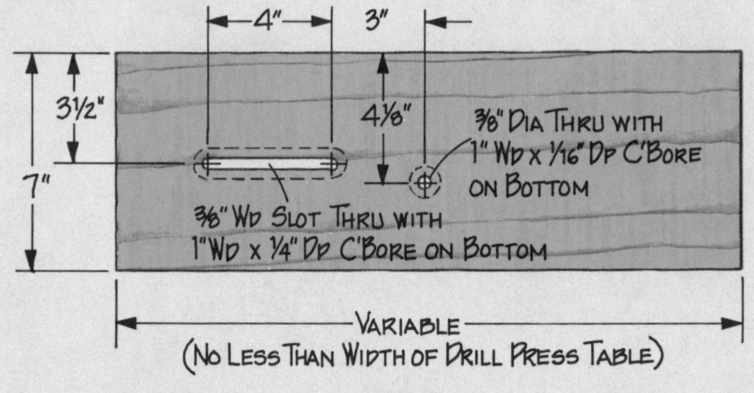
4"
3"
3½"
4⅛"
7"
⅜" Dia Thru with 1" Wd x 1/16" Dp C'Bore on Bottom
⅜" Wd Slot Thru with 1" Wd x ¼" Dp C'Bore on Bottom
Variable (No Less Than Width of Drill Press Table)

TOP VIEW
Base

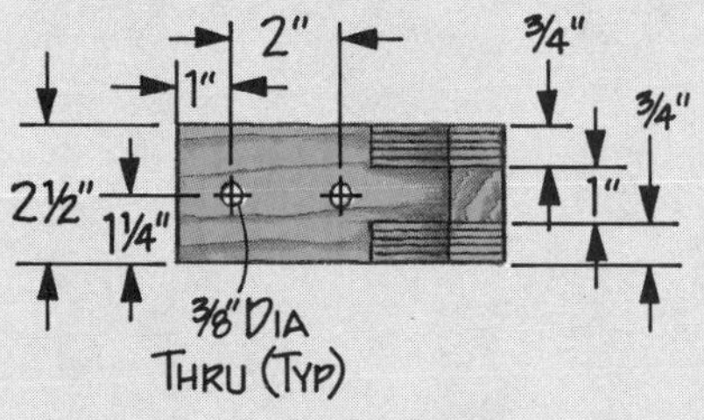
2"
1"
¾"
¾"
2½"
1¼"
1"
⅜" Dia Thru (Typ)

TOP VIEW

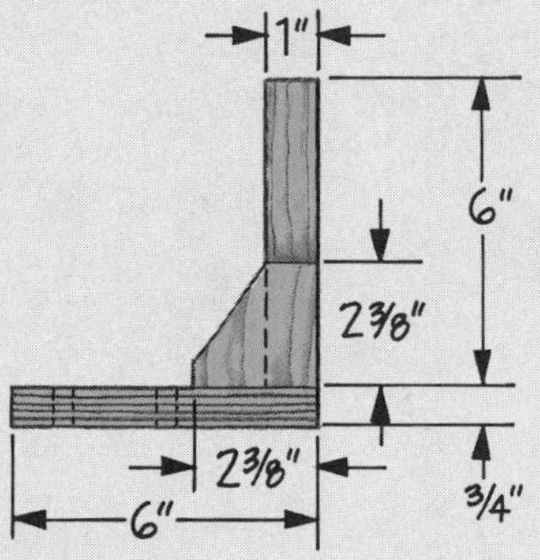
1"
6"
2⅜"
2⅜"
¾"
6"

FRONT VIEW
Tool Rest

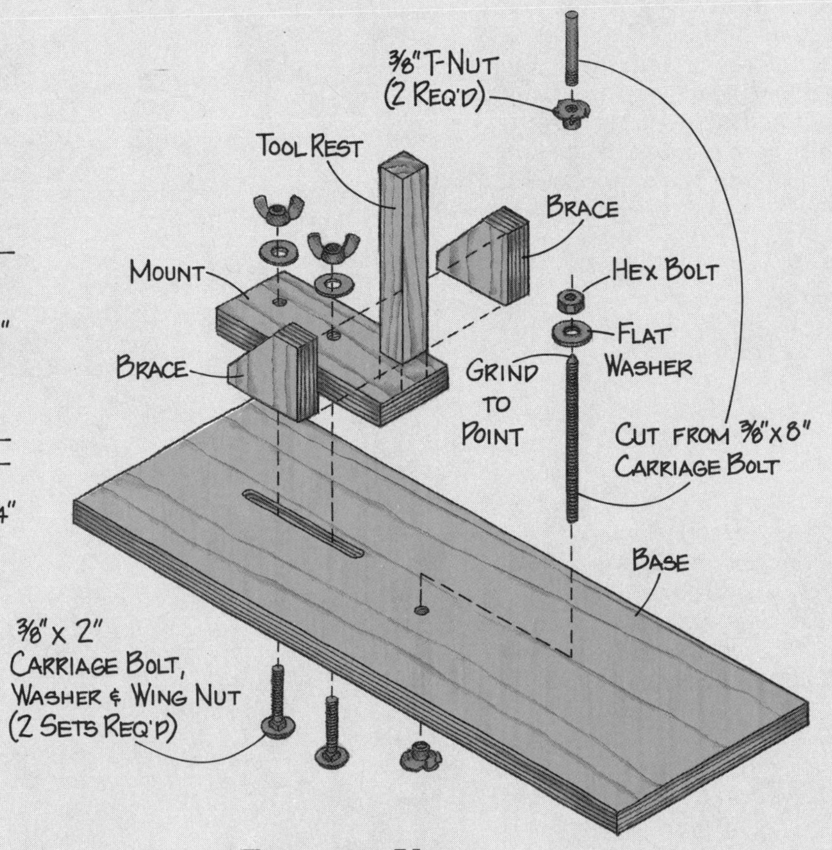
⅜" T-Nut (2 Req'd)
Tool Rest
Brace
Mount
Hex Bolt
Flat Washer
Brace
Grind to Point
Cut from ⅜" x 8" Carriage Bolt
Base
⅜" x 2" Carriage Bolt, Washer & Wing Nut (2 Sets Req'd)

Exploded View

Drill Press Turning Jig

PROJECTS

5

CARPENTER'S TOTE

A carpenter's tote is a portable tool box especially designed to hold the equipment a carpenter might need on the job. Its elongated shape will accommodate saws, yardsticks, pry bars, and other long tools. There is also ample room for hammers, screwdrivers, and smaller implements, a space for a router or another tall tool, and drawers for nails, drill bits, and other tiny items.

The outside shell of the tote is a six-board box with a cut-off lid. The parts of the box and drawer framework are all made from plywood. This cuts down on weight without sacrificing strength. Plywood is also more stable than solid wood, so there are no problems with expansion and contraction.

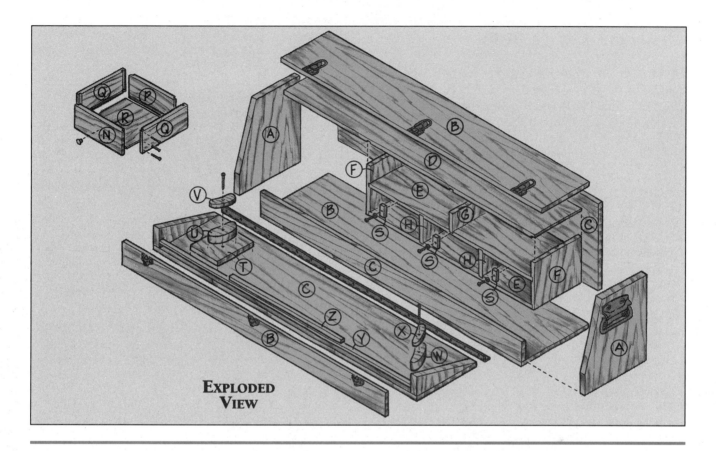

EXPLODED VIEW

MATERIALS LIST (FINISHED DIMENSIONS)

Parts

A. Ends* (2) $3/4'' \times 8^3/4'' \times 11''$

B. Top/bottom* (2) $1/2'' \times 9^3/4'' \times 37^1/2''$

C. Front/back* (2) $1/2'' \times 11'' \times 37^1/2''$

D. Drawer unit top* $1/2'' \times 7'' \times 36''$

E. Drawer unit middle/bottom* (2) $1/2'' \times 7'' \times 24''$

F. Drawer unit sides* (2) $1/2'' \times 7'' \times 6^1/4''$

G. Drawer unit top divider* $1/2'' \times 7'' \times 2^1/2''$

H. Drawer unit bottom dividers* (2) $1/2'' \times 7'' \times 3^1/2''$

J. Top drawer faces (2) $1/2'' \times 1^{15}/16'' \times 11^7/16''$

K. Top drawer backs (2) $1/2'' \times 1^{15}/16'' \times 10^{15}/16''$

L. Top drawer sides (4) $1/2'' \times 1^{15}/16'' \times 6^3/4''$

M. Top drawer bottoms* (2) $1/8'' \times 6^1/2'' \times 10^{15}/16''$

N. Bottom drawer faces (3) $1/2'' \times 2^{15}/16'' \times 7^7/16''$

P. Bottom drawer backs (3) $1/2'' \times 2^{15}/16'' \times 6^{15}/16''$

Q. Bottom drawer sides (6) $1/2'' \times 2^{15}/16'' \times 6^3/4''$

R. Bottom drawer bottoms* (3) $1/8'' \times 6^1/2'' \times 6^{15}/16''$

S. Drawer keepers (3) $3/8'' \times 1/2'' \times 1^1/2''$

T. Handsaw spacer $1/2'' \times 4'' \times 5''$

U. Handsaw holder $1'' \times$ (variable) x (variable)

V. Handsaw keeper $1/2'' \times$ (variable) x (variable)

W. Backsaw holder $1'' \times$ (Variable) x (variable)

X. Backsaw keeper $1/2'' \times$ (variable) x (variable)

Y. Long saw teeth protector $3/8'' \times 3/8'' \times 36''$

Z. Short saw teeth protector $3/8'' \times 3/8'' \times 16''$

Hardware

#8 x 1¼" Flathead wood screws (24–30)

#10 x 1½" Roundhead wood screws (5)

#10 Flat washers (5)

6d Finishing nails (24–36)

1" Wire brads (24–36)

1" x 36" Piano hinge and mounting screws

2¾" Draw catches and mounting screws (3)

1" Pulls (5)

Chest handles and mounting screws (2)

Make these parts from plywood.

PLAN OF PROCEDURE

1 Select the stock and cut the parts to size. To make this project, you need about 8 board feet of 4/4 (four-quarters) hardwood lumber, one-half sheet (4 feet by 4 feet) of cabinet-grade ½-inch plywood, and a few scraps of ¾-inch and ⅛-inch plywood. The carpenter's tote shown is made from poplar hardwood and birch plywood.

Plane the 4/4 lumber to ½ inch thick, then cut all the parts to the sizes listed in the Materials List, *except* for the drawer parts, the saw holders, and the saw keepers. Wait until after you have assembled the tote to make these parts.

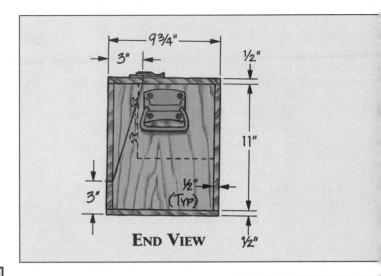

END VIEW

 FOR BEST RESULTS

Trim the visible edges of the plywood parts with hardwood to hide the plies. To do this, cut the top, bottom, front, and back ½ inch *shorter* than specified, and the drawer unit parts ¼ inch *narrower.* Glue ¼-inch-thick, ½-inch-wide hardwood strips to the ends of the top, bottom, front, and back, and to the front edges of the drawer unit parts.

2 Assemble the box and cut the lid. Mark the ends where you will cut off the lid. Using a saber saw, cut in about 1 inch from each edge along the lines you just marked. *(SEE FIGURE 5-1.)* Finish sand the inside surfaces of the top, bottom, front, back, and ends, then assemble them with glue and finishing nails. Be careful not to drive any nails where the lid will be cut free of the box — you might nick them with a saw blade.

After the glue dries, rip the top and front on a table saw. *(SEE FIGURE 5-2.)* Finish cutting the ends with a saber saw and remove the lid from the box. *(SEE FIGURE 5-3.)* Clean up the sawed edges with sandpaper or a file.

3 Cut the drawer unit joinery and assemble the parts. The framework that holds the drawers is assembled with ½-inch-wide, ¼-inch deep rabbets and dadoes. Cut these joints with a dado cutter or a router and a straight bit.

Finish sand the drawer unit parts, then put them together in this order:
- Attach the middle to the top divider.
- Attach the bottom to the bottom dividers.
- Join the middle assembly, bottom assembly, and sides.
- Attach the top to the sides and top divider.

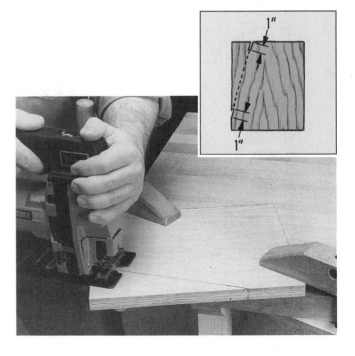

5-1 To separate the lid from the box, cut the top, front, and ends after the box is assembled. However, to maintain sharp angles and to keep from gouging the box parts, you must start the end cuts *before* you assemble the box. Cut in 1 inch from each edge with a saber saw.

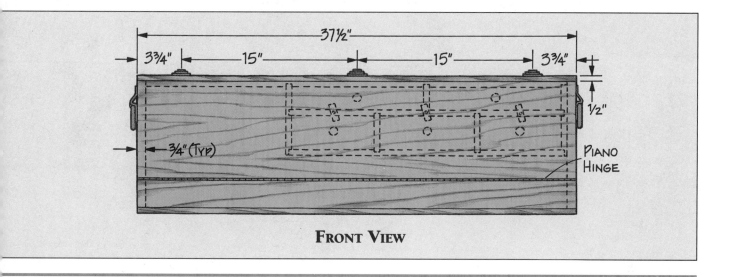

FRONT VIEW

Assemble each rabbet or dado with glue and flathead wood screws. Countersink the screws so the heads are flush with the wood surface.

4 Install the drawer unit in the box.   Glue the drawer unit to the top and the back of the box. To reinforce the glue joints, drive several flathead wood screws through the back and into the edges of the drawer unit. Countersink the screw heads.

Note: The top corner of the drawer unit should protrude slightly from the box. This will serve as a lip to keep the lid from shifting sideways.

5 Cut the drawer parts and the drawer joinery. Measure the opening in the drawer unit. If the dimensions have changed from what is shown on the working drawing, adjust the sizes of the drawer parts to compensate. Cut the drawer parts to size.

Cut the 1/4-inch-wide, 1/4-inch-deep rabbets and grooves in the drawer faces, backs, and sides with a dado cutter or a router and a straight bit. Make the 1/8-inch-wide, 1/4-inch-deep grooves that hold the drawer bottoms with a flat-ground rip saw blade. (Flat-ground saw teeth leave a kerf with a flat bottom, so the bottom surface is square to the sides.)

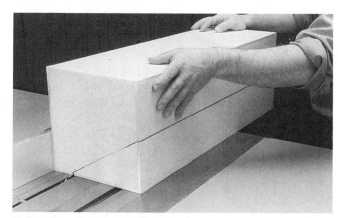

5-2 After the glue dries, rip the top and front on a table saw. Set the depth of cut to 1/2 inch — the teeth of the blade should just clear the stock as you cut. Position the rip fence 3 inches away from the blade. Make the cuts, using the fence to guide the box.

5-3 Use a saber saw to finish the cuts you started in the box ends. Cut one end, then tape it back together before you cut the second end — this will keep the lid from shifting as you complete the last cut. Remove the lid from the box and discard the tape.

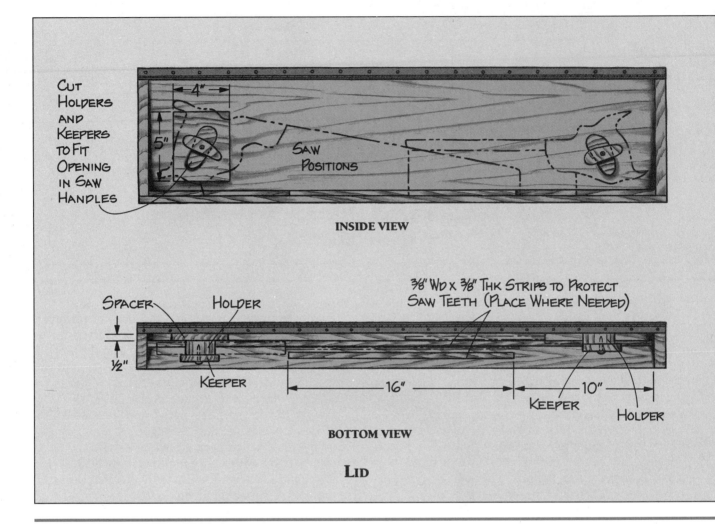

CUT HOLDERS AND KEEPERS TO FIT OPENING IN SAW HANDLES

4"

5"

SAW POSITIONS

INSIDE VIEW

SPACER   HOLDER

⅜" WD X ⅜" THK STRIPS TO PROTECT SAW TEETH (PLACE WHERE NEEDED)

½"

KEEPER

16"

10"

KEEPER

HOLDER

BOTTOM VIEW

LID

6 Assemble and fit the drawers. Finish sand the inside surfaces of the drawer parts. Assemble the drawer faces, backs, and sides with glue. As you put these together, slide the bottoms into their grooves. However, do *not* glue the bottoms in place; let them float.

After the glue dries, fit the drawers to their openings and install the drawer pulls. To keep from pulling the drawer faces off the drawer sides, reinforce the rabbet joints with wire brads.

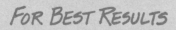

FOR BEST RESULTS

To get a good fit, build the drawers the same size as the openings. Sand or plane the outside surfaces of the assembled drawers until they slide smoothly in and out of the openings.

7 Install the saw holders and saw teeth protectors. If you wish to store saws in the lid, cut the holders and keepers to the same size and shape as the openings in the saw handles. Arrange the saw in the lid so the teeth rest against the top. With the saws in place, glue the spacer and holders to the inside surface of the front, as shown in the *Lid/Inside View*.

Note: If you use your handsaw more often than your backsaw, arrange the handsaw in front of the backsaw.

Let the glue dry, then position the long saw teeth protector between the two saws, and the short protector in front of the handsaw. There should be about ¼ inch between the two parts. Attach them to the top with glue. (These strips of wood not only keep the saws from banging into one another, they also help keep them in the lid.)

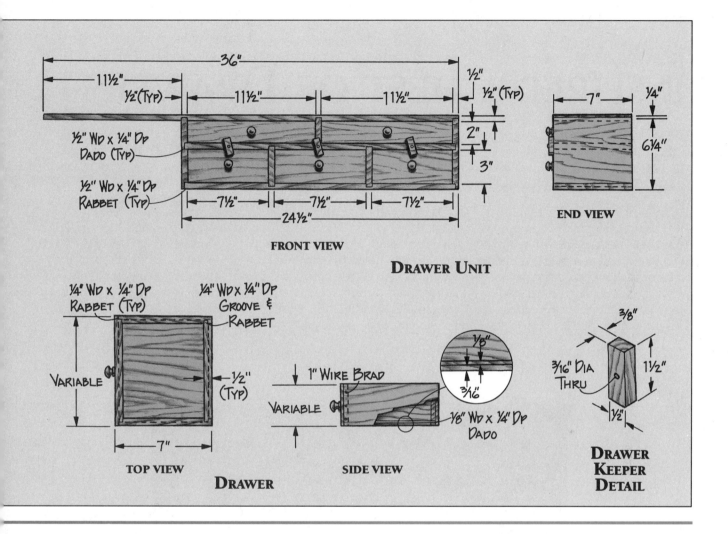

DRAWER UNIT

FRONT VIEW

END VIEW

½" WD x ¼" DP DADO (TYP)

½" WD x ¼" DP RABBET (TYP)

¼" WD x ¼" DP RABBET (TYP)

¼" WD x ¼" DP GROOVE & RABBET

VARIABLE

½" (TYP)

TOP VIEW

1" WIRE BRAD

VARIABLE

⅛" WD x ¼" DP DADO

SIDE VIEW

DRAWER

⅜"

3/16" DIA THRU

1½"

½"

DRAWER KEEPER DETAIL

8 **Install the keepers.** Drill 3/16-inch-diameter holes through the drawer keepers and saw keepers. Attach the drawer keepers to the front edges of the drawer unit with roundhead wood screws and washers, as shown in the *Drawer Unit/Front View.* (Just three keepers will prevent all five drawers from falling open.) Attach the saw keepers to the saw holders in the same manner.

9 **Attach the lid to the box.** Screw the piano hinge to the bottom edge of the lid, then attach the lid to the box. Close the lid and install draw catches on the top of the box.

10 **Finish the carpenter's tote.** Remove the lid, drawers, and keepers from the box and set the hardware aside. Apply a protective finish to all wood surfaces, inside and out. (The tote shown is finished with outdoor latex paint, but you can use any durable finish.) When the finish dries, replace the lid, drawers, and keepers. Finally, attach heavy-duty chest handles to the ends of the box.

FOR BEST RESULTS

Screws don't hold as well when driven into a plywood edge as they do when driven through the plies. To compensate for this, don't use the short mounting screws that come with most piano hinges. Instead substitute 1¼-inch-long screws of the same diameter to mount the hinge.

6

INSPIRED CHEST OF DRAWERS

Rick Goehring of Gambier, Ohio, builds "inspired" furniture. That is, his designs are inspired by eighteenth- and nineteeth-century craftsmen who worked and worshiped in Shaker, Amish, and Moravian religious communities. This contemporary chest of drawers is Shaker inspired, according to Rick.

Like the design, the construction of the chest is a blend of old and new, employing both nineteenth- and twentieth-century techniques. For example, a traditional case sits on a contemporary frame base, the front corners of which are joined by through dovetails.

"Furniture design has never been static," says Rick. "Folk furniture was always evolving; the builders were always trying something new. My pieces are just another step in this evolution."

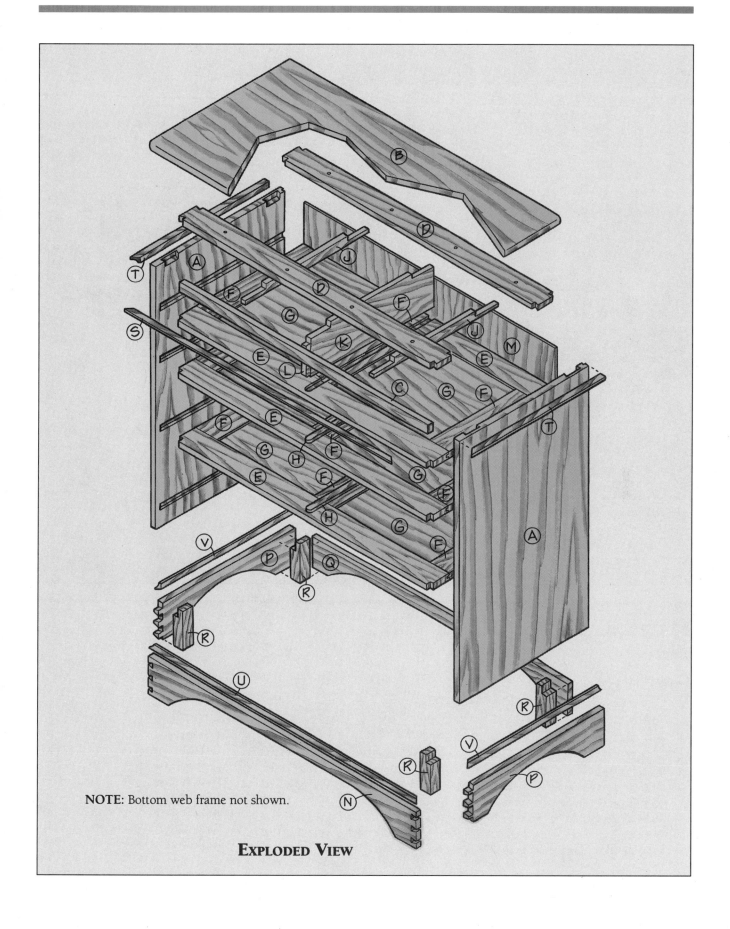

NOTE: Bottom web frame not shown.

EXPLODED VIEW

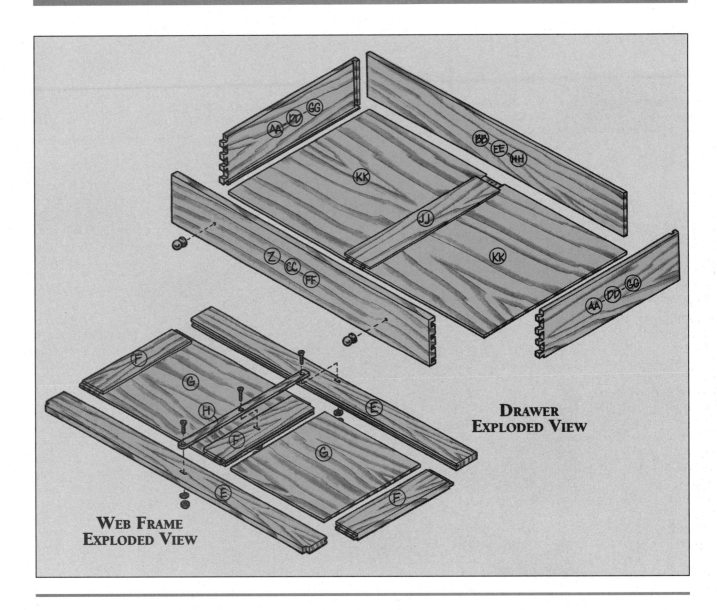

DRAWER EXPLODED VIEW

WEB FRAME EXPLODED VIEW

MATERIALS LIST (FINISHED DIMENSIONS)

Parts

Case

A. Case sides (2) 3/4″ x 20″ x 331/4″

B. Top   3/4″ x 21″ x 40″

C. Top rail   3/4″ x 11/4″ x 361/2″

D. Cleats* (2)   3/4″ x 3″ x 373/4″

E. Web frame stiles† (8)   3/4″ x 3″ x 371/4″

F. Web frame rails* (12)   3/4″ x 3″ x 141/4″

G. Dust panels‡ (8) 1/4″ x 141/4″ x 147/8″

H. Drawer guides* (3)   1/4″ x 1″ x 19″

J. Kickers* (2) 3/4″ x 11/4″ x 183/4″

K. Divider‡   3/4″ x 51/4″ x 183/4″

L. Divider front   3/4″ x 3/4″ x 4″

M. Back‡   1/4″ x 331/4″ x 371/4″

N. Base front   3/4″ x 43/4″ x 391/2″

P. Base sides (2)   3/4″ x 43/4″ x 203/4″

Q. Base back*   3/4″ x 4″ x 38″

R. Glue blocks* (4)   11/2″ x 11/2″ x 5″

S. Front top molding   3/4″ x 3/4″ x 391/2″

T. Side top moldings (2)   3/4″ x 3/4″ x 203/4″

U. Front base molding   1/2″ x 1/2″ x 39″

V. Side base moldings (2)   1/2″ x 1/2″ x 201/2″

MATERIALS LIST (FINISHED DIMENSIONS)

Parts — CONTINUED

Drawers

W. Top drawer
   fronts (2) $3/4'' \times 4'' \times 17^{7}/8''$

X. Top drawer
   sides* (4) $1/2'' \times 4'' \times 19^{5}/8''$

Y. Top drawer
   backs* (2) $1/2'' \times 3^{1}/2'' \times 17^{3}/8''$

Z. Top middle drawer
   front $3/4'' \times 6'' \times 36^{1}/2''$

AA. Top middle drawer
    sides* (2) $1/2'' \times 6'' \times 19^{5}/8''$

BB. Top middle drawer
    back* $1/2'' \times 5^{1}/2'' \times 36''$

CC. Bottom middle
    drawer front $3/4'' \times 8'' \times 36^{1}/2''$

DD. Bottom middle drawer
    sides* (2) $1/2'' \times 8'' \times 19^{5}/8''$

EE. Bottom middle drawer
    back* $1/2'' \times 7^{1}/2'' \times 36''$

FF. Bottom drawer
    front $3/4'' \times 10'' \times 36^{1}/2''$

GG. Bottom drawer
    sides* (2) $1/2'' \times 10'' \times 19^{5}/8''$

HH. Bottom drawer
    back* $1/2'' \times 9^{1}/2'' \times 36''$

JJ. Muntins*
    (3) $3/4'' \times 1^{3}/4'' \times 18^{3}/4''$

KK. Drawer bottoms‡
    (8) $1/4'' \times 17^{7}/8'' \times 18^{3}/4''$

Hardware

#8 x 1¼″ Flathead wood screws
   (36–40)

#10 x 2″ Flathead wood screws
   (12)

1″ Wire brads (48–60)

#8 x 1″ Flathead machine screws
   (9)

#8 Flat washers (9)

#8 Hex nuts (9)

Drawer pulls (8)

*Make these parts from a utility
hardwood.
†Make half of these parts from a
primary hardwood, and the other half
from a utility hardwood.
‡Make these parts from plywood.

PLAN OF PROCEDURE

1 Select the stock and cut the parts to size.
To make this project, you need about 32 board feet of 4/4 (four-quarters) *primary* hardwood (such as cherry or walnut), 32 board feet of 4/4 *utility* hardwood (such as maple or poplar), a 4-foot-by-8-foot sheet of ¼-inch cabinet-grade plywood, and small amounts of both 8/4 (eight-quarters) utility hardwood and ¾-inch plywood. You can use almost any pleasing combination of hardwoods and hardwood veneer plywood; however, Shakers traditionally favored cherry, maple, and poplar. For the chest of drawers shown, Rick used cherry and figured maple as the primary woods, maple as the utility wood, and birch-veneer plywood.

Plane the 4/4 lumber to ¾ inch thick, and the 8/4 lumber to 1½ inches thick. Cut the parts for the *case* to the sizes specified in the Materials List. Do *not* cut any other parts for the drawers yet; wait until after you have assembled the case.

2 Make the web frames. The web frame members are joined with tongue-and-groove joints. Cut ¼-inch-wide, ⅜-inch-deep grooves in the inside edges of the stiles and outside rails and in *both* edges of the middle rails. Cut ¼-inch-wide, ⅜-inch-long tongues in the ends of the rails to fit the grooves in the stiles. Cut ½-inch-wide, ⅜-inch-long notches in the outside corners of the front stiles, as shown in the *Web Frame Layout*.

Note: Make the front stiles from primary hardwood, since the outside edges of these parts will be visible on the assembled case. The other web frame members can be made from utility stock.

Give the web frame parts a light sanding, then assemble the rails and stiles with glue. As you put the parts together, slip the dust panels into the grooves. However, *don't* glue the panels in place; let them float.

FOR BEST RESULTS

The closer the frames are to being perfectly flat, the better the drawers will work. To make the frames as flat as possible, use clamps or weights to hold them down on a perfectly flat surface while the glue dries. If your workbench isn't flat enough for this purpose, use the work surface of your table saw. Lower the blade and spread a sheet of plastic over the saw to protect it from glue.

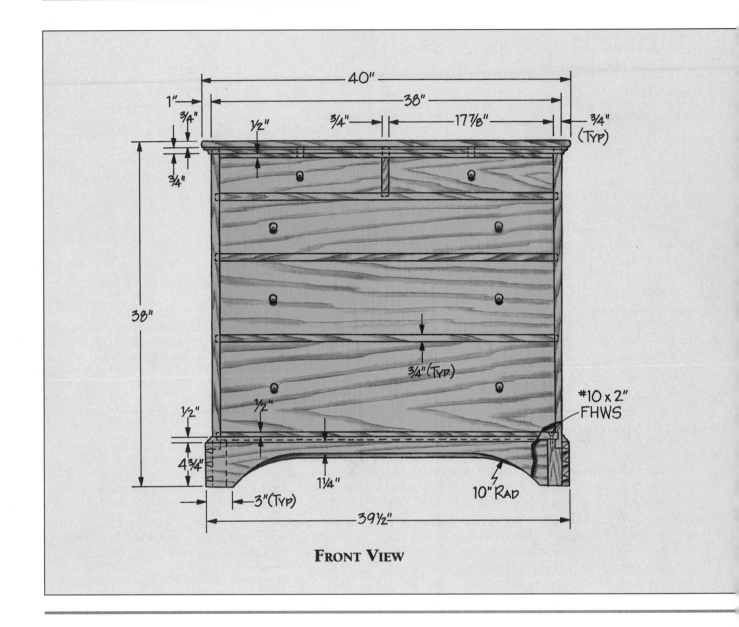

FRONT VIEW

Drill three 1-inch-diameter, ¼-inch-deep counterbores in the bottom surface of each web frame where you will attach the drawer guide. In the center of each counterbore, make a ³⁄₁₆-inch-wide slot running from side to side, as shown in the *Slot and Counterbore Detail.* Drill and countersink ⁵⁄₃₂-inch-diameter holes in the guides and attach them to the web frames with machine screws, as shown in the *Drawer Guide Mounting Detail.* The slots enable you to adjust the positions of the guides from side to side.

3 Cut the joinery in the sides, cleats, kickers, and divider. Using a band saw or dovetail saw, cut

dovetail tenons in the ends of the cleats, as shown in the *Cleat Layout.* Cut matching dovetail mortises in the top ends of the sides, as shown in the *Side Layout/ Top View.* Remove as much waste as you can from each mortise with a drill press and a Forstner bit, then clean up the mortise sides and bottoms with a hand chisel. Drill and countersink ⁵⁄₃₂-inch-diameter holes in the cleats to attach the top, and cut slots in the rear cleat to attach the divider and kickers.

Rout ¾-inch-wide, ³⁄₈-inch-deep blind dadoes in the sides, as shown in the *Side Layout/Side View.* Stop each dado ½ inch from the front edge, and square the blind end with a chisel. Also rout a ¼-inch-wide, ³⁄₈-inch-deep rabbet in the back edges.

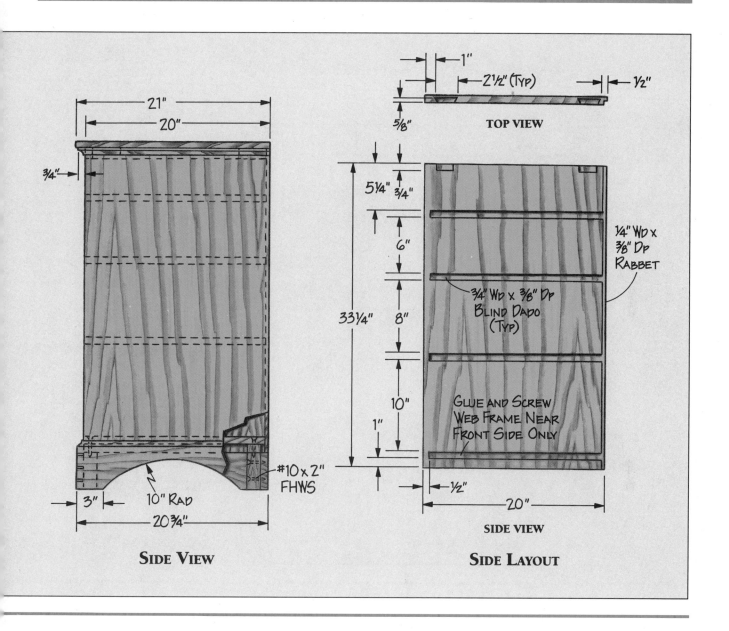

TOP VIEW

SIDE VIEW

SIDE LAYOUT

Lay out the shapes of the kickers and divider as shown in the *Kicker Layout* and *Divider Layout*. Cut the shapes with a band saw or saber saw.

4   Assemble the case.   Finish sand the sides, top, top rail, and divider front. Assemble the sides, cleats, web frames, and top rail with glue and #8 wood screws. Attach the web frames to the sides near the front edges *only*. Apply glue to just the front 2 or 3 inches of the dadoes, and anchor the web frames with flathead wood screws, as shown in the *Frame-to-Side Joinery Detail*. By leaving the rear portion of the frames unattached, you ensure that the sides can expand and contract.

Glue the cleats in their mortises, making sure to place the slotted cleat in the back. Attach the front ends of the kickers to the front cleat with glue, and the back ends to the back cleat with #8 wood screws. Glue the bottom edge and the top front corner of the divider in place, but fasten the back corner with a screw. (This arrangement will allow for expansion and contraction.) Attach the top, driving #8 wood screws up through the cleats and into the top. Temporarily tack the back to the case with wire brads, but don't drive them all the way in yet.

5   Build and attach the base.   Cut through dovetails to join the front corners of the base. Lay out the

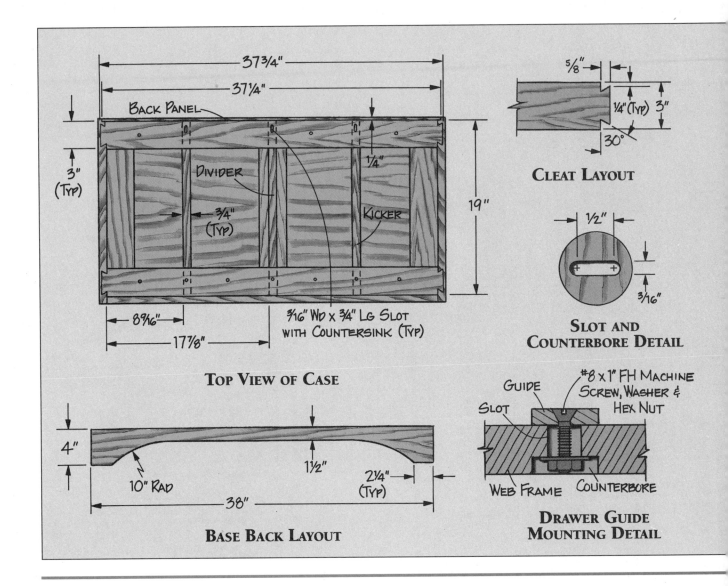

TOP VIEW OF CASE

CLEAT LAYOUT

SLOT AND COUNTERBORE DETAIL

BASE BACK LAYOUT

DRAWER GUIDE MOUNTING DETAIL

shapes of the feet on the base front, back, and sides, as shown in the *Front View, Side View,* and *Base Back Layout.* Cut the shapes with a band saw or saber saw, and sand the sawed edges. Also, cut notches in the top end of the glue blocks, as shown in the *Glue Block Layout.*

Finish sand the base parts. Assemble the base front, back, sides, and glue blocks with glue. Reinforce the back glue blocks by driving #10 wood screws through the blocks and into the back and sides. Let the glue dry, then sand the joints flush. Set the case on the base, remove the back, and drive #10 wood screws down through the bottom web frame and into the glue blocks. Countersink the screws so the heads are slightly *below* the frame surface. Replace the back and drive the brads home.

6 Attach the moldings to the case. Pick clear primary stock for the moldings, and plane the base molding stock to 1/2 inch thick. (Leave the top molding stock 3/4 inch thick.) Rout or cut the shape of the top moldings in the edge of the 3/4-inch-thick stock, as shown in the *Top Molding Profile,* and the base moldings in the 1/2-inch-thick stock, as shown in the *Base Molding Profile.* Rip the shaped edges from the boards to make the moldings.

Finish sand the molding stock. Cut the moldings to length, mitering the adjoining ends. Attach the base moldings to the top edges of the base with glue and wire brads — *don't* glue them to the sides or the bottom web frame. (This will allow you to remove the base, should it ever be necessary.)

Attach the top moldings to the sides and the front

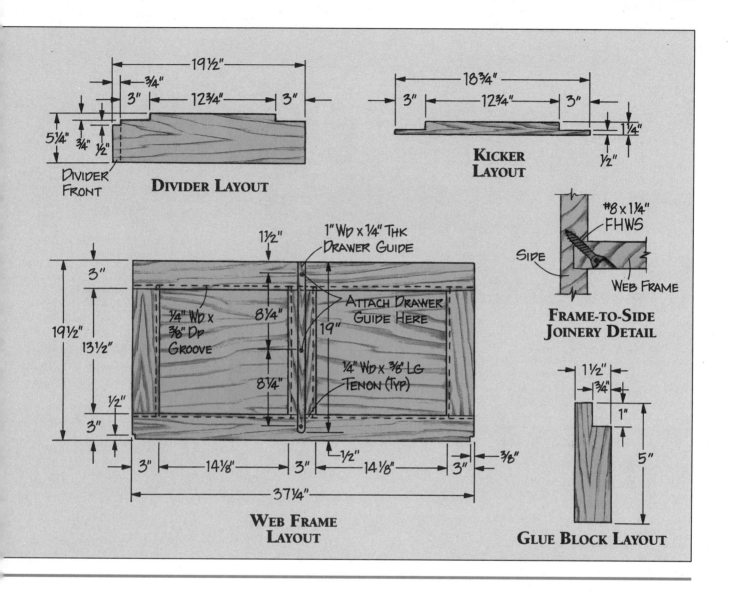

DIVIDER LAYOUT

KICKER LAYOUT

WEB FRAME LAYOUT

FRAME-TO-SIDE JOINERY DETAIL

GLUE BLOCK LAYOUT

rail with wire brads. You can glue the top front molding to the top rail, and the top side moldings to the front 3 inches of the sides. However, *don't* glue the top moldings to the top. And don't glue the top side moldings to the back portion of the sides; just attach these moldings to the sides with brads. As the sides expand and contract, the brads will bend slightly.

7 Cut the drawer joinery. Measure the drawer openings in the assembled case. If the dimensions have changed from what is shown in the working drawings, adjust the sizes of the drawer parts to compensate. Cut the ³/₄-inch-thick parts — the drawer faces and the muntins. Plane the utility stock to ¹/₂ inch thick, then cut the remaining drawer parts to size.

Cut half-blind dovetails to join the front corners of

the drawers, and ¹/₂-inch-wide, ¹/₄-inch-deep dadoes to join the back corners. To hold the drawer bottoms, make ¹/₄-inch-wide, ¹/₄-inch-deep grooves in the edges of the muntins and the inside surfaces of the drawer faces and sides. Also make 1-inch-wide, ¹/₄-inch-deep grooves in the bottom faces of the muntins, as shown in the *Muntin Detail/End View,* to ride over the drawer guides. Cut ¹/₄-inch-thick, ¹/₄-inch-long tenons in the front ends of the muntins and ⁵/₈-inch-thick, ¹/₂-inch-long tenons in the back ends, as shown in the *Muntin Detail/Side View.*

8 Assemble and fit the drawers. Finish sand the parts of each drawer, then assemble the drawer face, sides, back, and muntin with glue. Reinforce the glue joint between the muntin and the back by driving

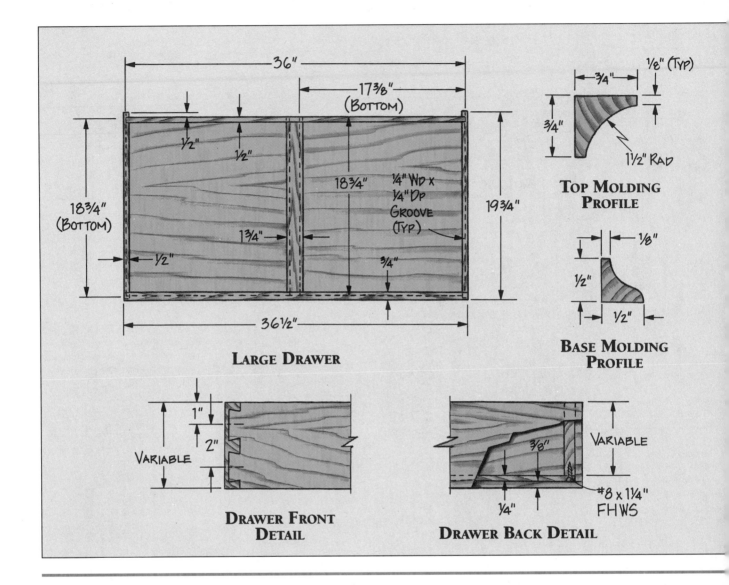

LARGE DRAWER

TOP MOLDING PROFILE

BASE MOLDING PROFILE

DRAWER FRONT DETAIL

DRAWER BACK DETAIL

a #8 wood screw up through the muntin tongue and into the back. Countersink the screw so the head is slightly below the bottom of the 1-inch-wide groove in the muntin. Slide the drawer bottoms into place and attach them to the back with #8 wood screws.

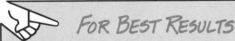

FOR BEST RESULTS

Like the web frames, the drawers must be perfectly flat. Use clamps or weights to hold them down on a flat surface while the glue dries.

Let the glue cure overnight, then sand the joints flush. Attach drawer pulls and test fit the drawers in

their openings. Adjust the side-to-side position of the drawer guides until they align with the 1-inch-wide grooves in the muntins. Shave the sides of these bottom grooves with a file until they slip over the guides with very little play. Sand or plane the sides and top edges of the drawers until they slide in and out of the case smoothly. Remember to fit the drawers for the time of year — close in the summer, loose in the winter. **Note:** As specified in the Materials List and the working drawings, the assembled drawer will be the same size as the openings. This, of course, is too big — eventually, you will have to make them slightly smaller than the openings. However, it's much easier to get a good fit if you build the drawers to the size of the openings, then plane or sand the surfaces until they slide in and out of the chest smoothly.

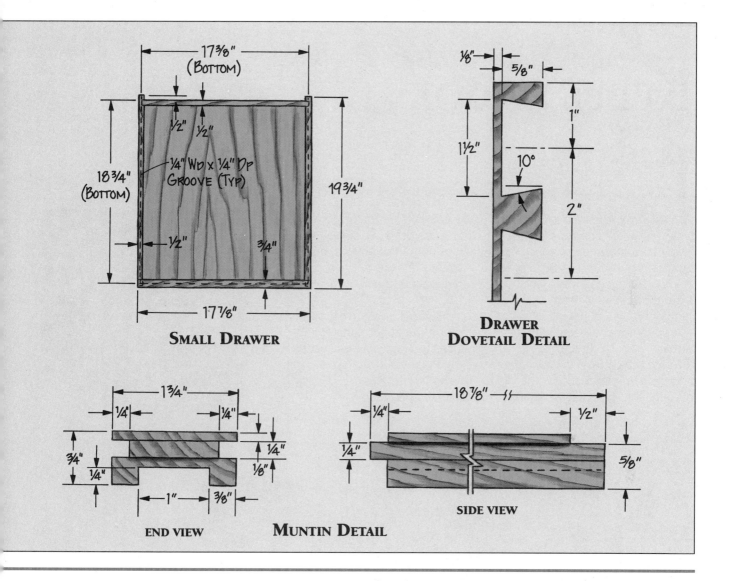

SMALL DRAWER

DRAWER DOVETAIL DETAIL

END VIEW   **MUNTIN DETAIL**

SIDE VIEW

9 **Finish the chest of drawers.** Remove the drawers from the case. If you used metal pulls, remove them from the drawers and set them aside. Do any necessary touch-up sanding, then apply a finish. Coat all the surfaces of the case, inside and out, to help prevent the wide parts — the sides and top — from cupping or checking.

To finish the drawers in a traditional manner, apply finish to the outside surface of the fronts, but leave the remaining surfaces unfinished. Or, if you prefer, finish all the surfaces, inside and out.

When the finish dries, rub it out and apply a coat of paste wax to the outside surfaces. To help the drawers slide smoothly, wax the drawer guides and the bottom edges of the drawers. Replace the drawer pulls and put the drawers back in the chest.

A BIT OF ADVICE

Think about what you will be storing in the drawers before you decide to finish the interior surfaces. Many finishes give off an odor long after they've cured, and they may impart chemical odors to foodstuffs, linens, or clothes.

7

KEEPING BOX

arly Americans referred to certain small chests as *keeping boxes*. It's a fitting description; hundreds of things can be kept in a box this size, including jewelry, hand tools, silverware, and stationery.

A problem with keeping boxes is that it may be difficult to root through the entire contents only to find the item you need is at the very bottom. This box helps organize the contents by tucking two more boxes inside — a drawer that slides out of the bottom, and a tray that lifts out of the top.

The box is joined at the corners with finger joints. The drawer face is ripped from the box front *after* making the finger joints, and it retains its fingers on both ends. When you close the drawer, the fingers interlock so the drawer is barely visible.

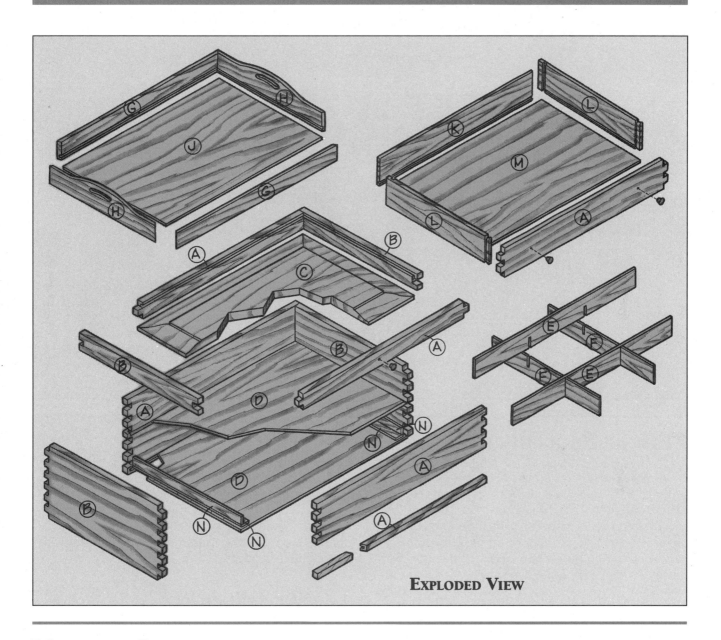

EXPLODED VIEW

MATERIALS LIST (FINISHED DIMENSIONS)

Parts

A. Front/back (2) $\frac{1}{2}$" x 8" x 17"

B. Sides (2) $\frac{1}{2}$" x 8" x 12"

C. Top $\frac{5}{8}$" x $11\frac{3}{8}$" x $16\frac{1}{2}$"

D. Middle/bottom*
   (2) $\frac{1}{4}$" x $11\frac{1}{2}$" x $16\frac{1}{2}$"

E. Long
   dividers (2) $\frac{1}{8}$" x $1\frac{3}{4}$" x 16"

F. Short
   dividers (2) $\frac{1}{8}$" x $1\frac{3}{4}$" x 11"

G. Tray front/
   back (2) $\frac{1}{4}$" x $1\frac{1}{2}$" x $15\frac{7}{8}$"

H. Tray sides (2) $\frac{1}{4}$" x 2" x $10\frac{7}{8}$"

J. Tray
   bottom* $\frac{1}{8}$" x $10\frac{5}{8}$" x $15\frac{5}{8}$"

K. Drawer
   back $\frac{1}{4}$" x $2\frac{3}{8}$" x $15\frac{1}{2}$"

L. Drawer
   sides (2) $\frac{1}{4}$" x $2\frac{3}{8}$" x $11\frac{3}{8}$"

M. Drawer
   bottom* $\frac{1}{8}$" x $10\frac{5}{8}$" x $15\frac{1}{2}$"

N. Drawer
   spacers (4) $\frac{1}{8}$" x $\frac{3}{4}$" x 11"

Hardware

Hidden barrel hinges (2)

Mortised lid supports (2)

$\frac{3}{8}$" Pulls (3)

Jewelry box feet (4)

Make these parts from plywood.

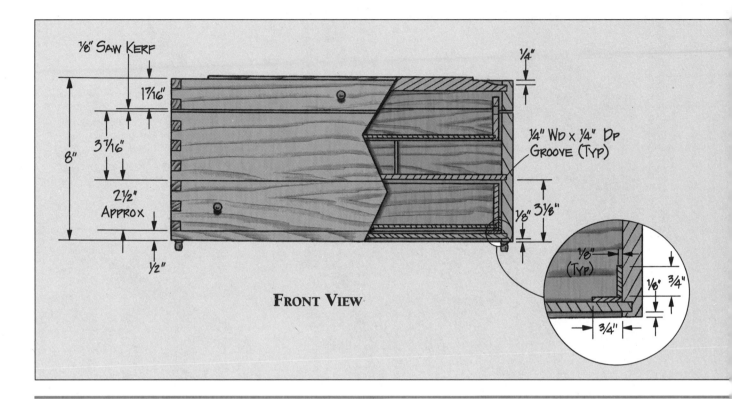

FRONT VIEW

PLAN OF PROCEDURE

1 Select the stock and cut the parts to size.
To make this project, you need about 7 board feet of 4/4 (four-quarters) hardwood and some large scraps of cabinet-grade ¼-inch and ⅛-inch plywood. The plywood veneer should match or complement the hardwood. If not, purchase matching veneer to cover the plywood. The keeping box shown is made from mahogany lumber and birch plywood; the plywood is faced with mahogany veneer.

Set aside some of the 4/4 lumber to resaw for the thin parts, then plane the rest to ⅝ inch thick and cut the top. Plane the stock again and cut the ½-inch-thick parts to size. Resaw the 4/4 lumber you set aside, splitting the wood in half. Plane each half to ¼ inch thick and cut the tray and drawer parts. Set aside some ¼-inch-thick stock to use for test pieces and plane the remainder to ⅛ inch thick. From this, cut the dividers and drawer spacers.

2 Cut the box joinery. Cut ½-inch-wide, ½-inch-long finger joints in the adjoining ends of the box front, back, and sides. Rout ¼-inch-wide, ¼-inch-deep grooves in the inside surfaces of these parts to hold the top, middle, and bottom, as shown in the *Front View*.

Whenever one of these grooves continues on into a finger, you must make the groove *blind* — stop routing ¼ inch before you reach the end of the finger. Square the blind ends with a chisel. (If you cut the grooves through to the ends, they will be visible when you assemble the box.)

3 Separate the drawer front. Rip the box front into three parts. Make the top part 5 inches wide and the bottom part ½ inch wide. The middle part, which will be approximately 2½ inches wide (minus the saw kerfs), will become the drawer front. To keep the kerfs as small as possible, use a band saw with a ⅛-inch blade or a scroll saw with a thin blade to do this ripping. (*SEE FIGURE 7-1.*) If you use a table saw, the kerfs will be too wide and there will be unsightly gaps between the box front and the drawer front.

4 Raise the panel. Using a table-mounted router or a shaper, cut an ogee shape all around the perimeter of the top to raise the center, as shown in the *Top Panel Detail*. If you wish, you can use another shape such as a radius or a simple bevel. Or, make a *flat* panel from ¼-inch-thick stock.

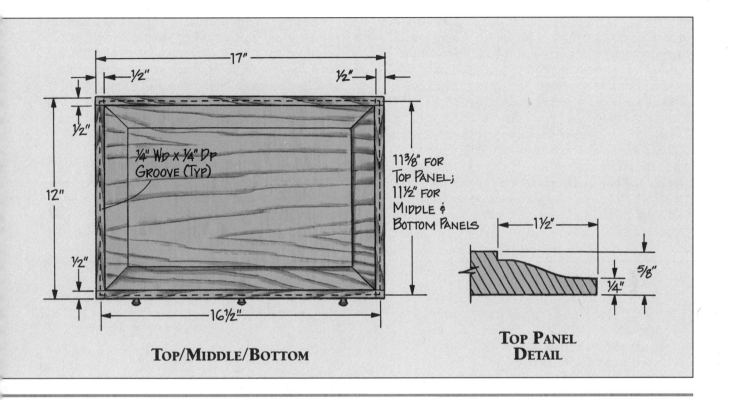

¼" Wd x ¼" Dp
Groove (Typ)

17"

½"   ½"

½"

12"

½"

16½"

11⅜" for
Top Panel;
11½" for
Middle &
Bottom Panels

TOP/MIDDLE/BOTTOM

1½"

5/8"

¼"

**TOP PANEL
DETAIL**

5 **Assemble the box and cut the lid.** Finish sand the box front pieces, sides, back, top, middle, and bottom. Assemble the front pieces, sides, and back with glue. As you do so, slide the top, middle, and bottom into place. *Don't* glue these parts in their grooves; let them float.

Let the glue dry overnight, and sand the finger joints flush. Rip the lid from the box on a table saw, using the fence to guide the cut. Adjust the depth of cut so you don't quite slice all the way through the ½-inch-thick box parts; leave about 1/32 inch remaining. Cut through the last little bit of stock with a utility knife, then trim away the tabs with sandpaper or a file.

7-1 Although it's not commonly used for this purpose, you can use a scroll saw to rip a board. You cannot use a fence — the thin blade will drift in the cut if you do. Instead, make the cut slowly and carefully by hand, following the mark as precisely as possible. To make the kerf as small and as smooth as possible, use a blade about .018 inch wide with 10 to 12 teeth per inch.

6 **Install the hinges and lid supports.** Both the hinges and the lid supports are hidden in holes and mortises so you won't be able to see any portion of them when the lid is closed.

Drill mortises for the hinges first. Carefully position the lid on the box and mark the positions of the hinges

on the back. Draw the lines across the cut so both the lid and the box are marked identically. Using a small square, transfer these lines to the back edges of the box and lid. At each mark, drill a stopped hole, centered in the edge. **Note:** The diameter and depth of the hinge holes depends on the make of the barrel hinges. Carefully measure the barrels before drilling.

Mark the positions of the lid supports on the sides. Drill holes in the bottom edges of the lid sides to attach the support arms. Rout mortises in the top edges of the box sides to hold the support housings. (*SEE FIGURE 7-2.*) **Note:** The sizes and positions of the holes and mortises will depend on the make of the lid supports.

WHERE TO FIND IT

The barrel hinges and mortised lid supports are available from:

The Woodworkers' Store
21801 Industrial Boulevard
Rogers, MN 55374-9514

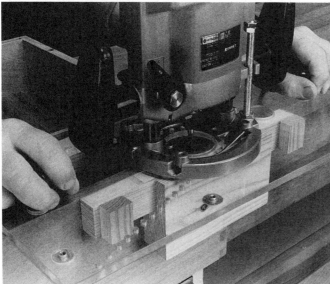

7-2 To rout the mortises for the lid supports, you must balance your router on the top edges of the box and make a perfectly straight cut, stopping when the mortise is just the right length. To help do this, first attach your router to an extended router base — a large piece of acrylic plastic or plywood. Make a fence with stops and attach it to the bottom surface of the extended base with double-faced carpet tape. Also make and attach a guide to the box with tape. The extended base will help you balance the router. The fence and the guide will keep the router moving in a straight line, and the stops will halt the cut automatically.

7 Assemble the dividers. Using a table saw and a flat-ground rip blade, cut kerfs in the dividers, as shown in the *Long Divider Layout* and the *Short Divider Layout*. (These kerfs become narrow lap joints when the dividers are assembled into a grid.) Finish sand the dividers and glue them together. Insert the grid in the box so it rests on the middle, but *don't* glue it in place. Leave the grid loose so you can remove it to facilitate cleaning inside the box.

8 Assemble the tray. Make miter joints in the adjoining ends of the tray front, back, and sides, and rout 1/8-inch-wide, 1/8-inch-deep grooves in the inside surfaces to hold the tray bottom. Cut the shape of the tray sides on a scroll saw or with a coping saw, as shown in the *Tray Side Pattern*. Finish sand the tray parts, then assemble the front, back, and sides with glue. As you do so, slide the bottom into its grooves, but don't glue it in place.

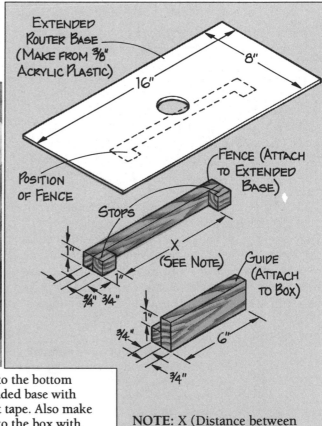

NOTE: X (Distance between stops) equals 6″ (length of guide) plus length of mortise minus diameter of bit.

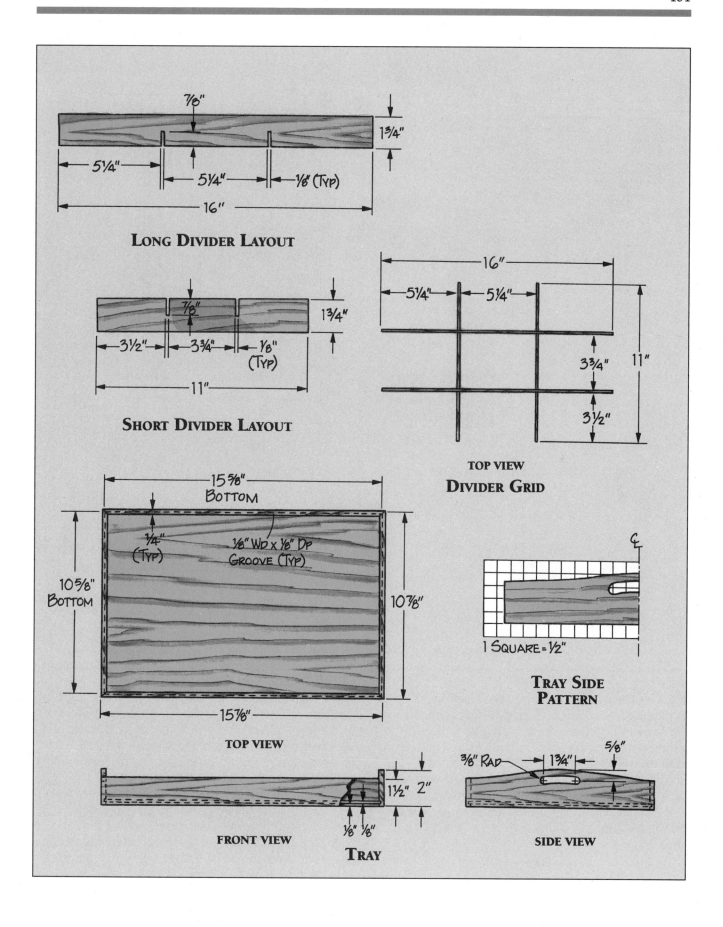

LONG DIVIDER LAYOUT

SHORT DIVIDER LAYOUT

TOP VIEW
DIVIDER GRID

TOP VIEW

1 SQUARE = 1/2"

TRAY SIDE
PATTERN

FRONT VIEW
TRAY

SIDE VIEW

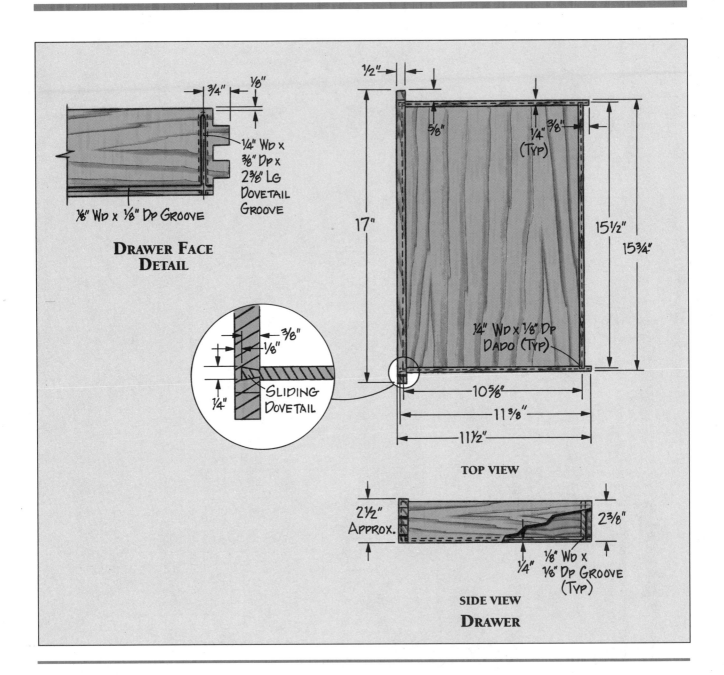

DRAWER FACE DETAIL

¾" WD x ⅜" DP x 2⅜" LG DOVETAIL GROOVE

⅛" WD x ⅛" DP GROOVE

SLIDING DOVETAIL

½"

5⅛"

¼" ⅜" (TYP)

17"

15½"

15¾"

¼" WD x ⅛" DP DADO (TYP)

10⅝"

11⅜"

11½"

TOP VIEW

2½" APPROX.

2⅜"

¼" ⅛" WD x ⅛" DP GROOVE (TYP)

SIDE VIEW DRAWER

9 **Cut the drawer joinery.** Rout sliding dovetails to join the front corners of the drawers, as shown in the *Drawer/Top View.* When making the dovetail grooves in the drawer front, stop the grooves ⅛ inch from the top edge, as shown in the *Drawer Face Detail.* Rout ¼-inch-wide, ⅛-inch-deep dadoes to join the back corners, and ⅛-inch-wide, ⅛-inch-deep grooves in the inside surfaces of the drawer parts to hold the drawer bottom.

10 **Assemble and fit the drawer.** Finish sand the drawer parts and glue the drawer front, sides, and back together. As you assemble the drawer, slide the bottom into its grooves but do *not* glue it in place. Also, glue the drawer spacers inside the drawer opening in the box, as shown in the *Front View.*

After the glue dries, install pulls on the drawer front. Test the fit of the drawer in its opening. If it binds, carefully sand or plane the drawer surfaces until it slides smoothly in and out of the box. Remember, the fingers on the ends of the drawer front must interlock with the fingers on the sides.

11 **Finish the box.** Remove the divider grid and drawer from the box. Do any necessary touch-up sanding, then apply a finish to all wooden surfaces, inside and out. Let the finish dry, rub it out, and apply a coat of paste wax. Wax the drawer spacers, too — this will help the drawer slide smoothly.

If you wish, cover the bottom of the drawer, the tray, and the well inside the box with felt or velvet. This will help protect fine items you wish to store in the box, as well as give the interior of the box a more finished look.

Replace the lid, grid, and drawer, and install the hinges, supports, and pulls. Also attach brass feet to the bottom of the box. Finally, set the tray inside the box on top of the divider grid.

TRY THIS TRICK

To fit the fabric lining in the drawer, cover the bottom surface of the material with carpet tape and cut the pieces to size with scissors or a utility knife. (The tape stiffens the fabric, making it easier to cut and fit.) To install the lining, simply peel the paper backing off the tape and press the fabric in place.

VARIATIONS

You can adapt this keeping box to store almost any kind of small item by rearranging the dividers inside the box or adding dividers in the drawer and the tray. Make these dividers from 1/8-inch-thick stock in the same manner that you made the grid for inside the box well.

You can also add more trays to the box. For example, the drawer will hold a small tray. Or, divide the tray at the top of the box into two shallower trays, stacked one on top of the other.

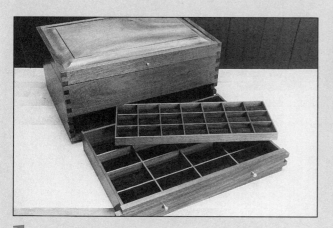

1 **Make a small tray to fit** inside the drawer, then rest it on dividers. To reach the items under this tray, slide it out of the way or lift it out of the drawer.

2 **Make two shallow trays to** fit in the top of the box instead of one deep tray. Design the trays so they stack on one another. The bottom tray shown has a handle in the center that extends up through an opening in the top tray. This enables you to lift both trays at once and quickly reach the items stored in the bottom of the well.

8

APOTHECARY HIGHBOY

Apothecaries, or old-time pharmacists, once used chests full of dozens of small drawers to organize their healing herbs, powders, and chemicals. These storage units became known as apothecary chests. Today, apothecary chests are much sought after by antique collectors — the diminutive drawers are still useful to help organize small household items.

However, as most owners of antique apothecary chests admit, all those small drawers can be too much of a good thing. A chest with several different sizes of drawers is more practical for most homes. The mix of drawer sizes lets you organize and store all sorts of items.

Earlier in the 1900s, Robert Dodson, a country craftsman in Tipp City, Ohio, designed a "false-front apothecary chest" for a client who wanted to have his chest and use it, too. At first glance, this piece appears to be a traditional apothecary chest. However, many of the drawers have shaped fronts that make them look like two or more smaller drawers. In reality, there are six different sizes of drawers in this chest. The drawers, in fact, are laid out more like a highboy than an apothecary chest.

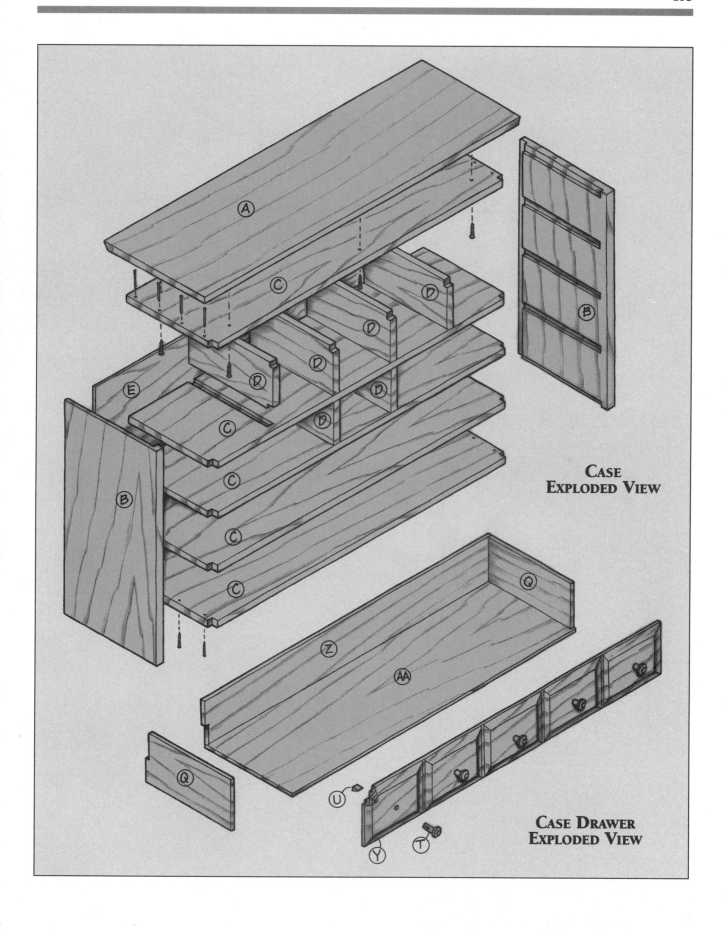

**CASE
EXPLODED VIEW**

**CASE DRAWER
EXPLODED VIEW**

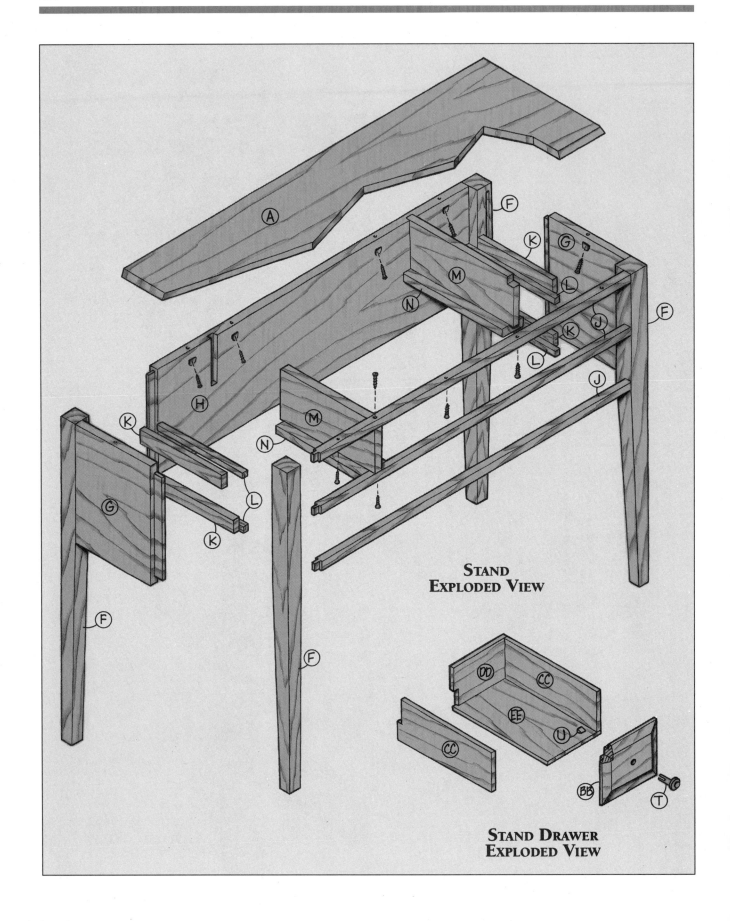

**STAND
EXPLODED VIEW**

**STAND DRAWER
EXPLODED VIEW**

Materials List (FINISHED DIMENSIONS)

Parts

Case

A. Top   3/4" x 12" x 37 7/8"
B. Sides (2)   3/4" x 11 1/4" x 23 1/4"
C. Shelves (5)   3/4" x 11" x 35 3/8"
D. Case dividers (6)   3/4" x 11" x 5 3/8"
E. Back*   1/4" x 23 1/4" x 35 7/8"

Stand

A. Top   3/4" x 12" x 37 7/8"
F. Legs (4)   1 5/8" x 1 5/8" x 30"
G. Side aprons (2)   3/4" x 10 1/4" x 9 1/2"
H. Back apron   3/4" x 10 1/4" x 34 5/8"
J. Front rails (3)   3/4" x 3/4" x 34 5/8"
K. Drawer guides (4)   7/8" x 2" x 8"
L. Outside drawer supports (4)   3/4" x 3/4" x 9 3/4"
M. Stand dividers (2)   3/4" x 10 3/4" x 4 3/4"
N. Inside drawer supports (2)   3/4" x 2 1/4" x 9 3/4"

Small Case Drawers (Make 6)

P. Small case drawer fronts (6)   7/8" x 5 3/8" x 6 7/8"
Q. Case drawer sides (12)   3/8" x 4 7/8" x 10 1/2"
R. Small case drawer backs (6)   3/8" x 4 7/8" x 6 3/8"
S. Small case drawer bottoms* (6)   1/4" x 6" x 10 1/8"
T. Drawer pulls (6)   1 1/4" dia. x 2 1/2"
U. Wedges (6)   5/16" x 5/8" x 3/4"

Medium Case Drawers (Make 2)

Q. Case drawer sides (4)   3/8" x 4 7/8" x 10 1/2"
T. Drawer pulls (4)   1 1/4" dia. x 2 1/2"
U. Wedges (4)   5/16" x 5/8" x 3/4"
V. Medium case drawer fronts (2)   7/8" x 5 3/8" x 14"
W. Medium case drawer backs (2)   3/8" x 4 7/8" x 13 1/2"
X. Medium case drawer bottoms* (2)   1/4" x 10 1/8" x 13 1/8"

Large Case Drawers (Make 2)

Q. Case drawer sides (4)   3/8" x 4 7/8" x 10 1/2"
T. Drawer pulls (10)   1 1/4" dia. x 2 1/2"
U. Wedges (10)   5/16" x 5/8" x 3/4"
Y. Large case drawer fronts (2)   7/8" x 5 3/8" x 35 3/8"
Z. Large case drawer backs (2)   3/8" x 4 7/8" x 34 7/8"
AA. Large case drawer bottoms* (2)   1/4" x 10 1/8" x 34 1/2"

Small Stand Drawers (Make 2)

T. Drawer pulls (2)   1 1/4" dia. x 2 1/2"
U. Wedges (2)   5/16" x 5/8" x 3/4"
BB. Small stand drawer fronts (2)   7/8" x 4 1/2" x 5 7/8"
CC. Stand drawer sides (4)   3/8" x 4" x 10 1/2"
DD. Small stand drawer backs (2)   3/8" x 4" x 5 3/8"
EE. Small stand drawer bottoms* (2)   1/4" x 5" x 10 1/8"

Medium Stand Drawer (Make 1)

T. Drawer pulls (2)   1 1/4" dia. x 2 1/2"
U. Wedges (2)   5/16" x 5/8" x 3/4"
CC. Stand drawer sides (2)   3/8" x 4" x 10 1/2"
FF. Medium stand drawer front   7/8" x 4 1/2" x 21 3/8"
GG. Medium stand drawer back   3/8" x 4" x 20 7/8"
HH. Medium stand drawer bottom*   1/4" x 10 1/8" x 20 1/2"

Large Stand Drawer (Make 1)

T. Drawer pulls (2)   1 1/4" dia. x 2 1/2"
U. Wedges (2)   5/16" x 5/8" x 3/4"
CC. Stand drawer sides (2)   3/8" x 4" x 10 1/2"
JJ. Large stand drawer front   7/8" x 4 1/2" x 33 5/8"
KK. Large stand drawer back   3/8" x 4" x 33 1/8"
LL. Large stand drawer bottom*   1/4" x 10 1/8" x 32 3/4"

Hardware

7/8" Wire brads (24–30)
3d Finishing nails (1/2 lb.)
#8 x 1 1/4" Roundhead wood screws (6)
#8 x 1 1/4" Flathead wood screws (40)

*Make these parts from plywood.

Plan of Procedure

1 **Select the stock and cut the parts to size.**
To make this project, you need about 65 board feet of 4/4 (four-quarters) stock — 30 board feet of primary wood and 35 of a utility wood. You also need 8 board feet of 8/4 (eight-quarters) stock, and one full sheet of

1/4-inch plywood. You can use almost any cabinet-grade wood; however, the chest shown is made from cherry and pine.

Resaw 15 board feet of the 4/4 utility stock in half and plane it to 3/8 inch thick. Set it aside. Later, you'll

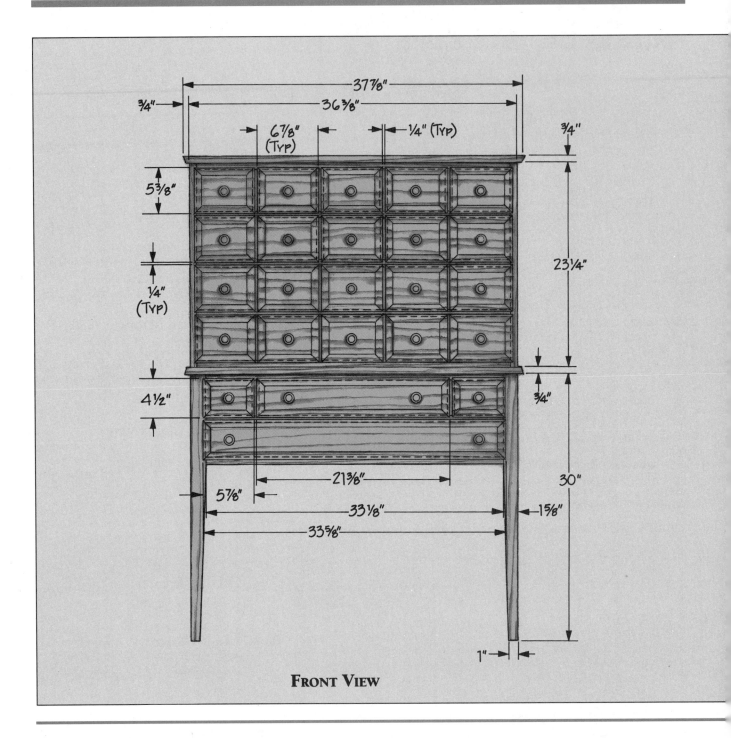

FRONT VIEW

make the drawer backs and sides from this. Plane the remaining 4/4 stock (both primary and utility) to ⅞ inch thick. Cut the drawer guides to the sizes specified in the Materials List. Set aside enough lumber to make the drawer fronts, but don't cut them to size yet. Plane the remaining ⅞-inch-thick lumber to ¾ inch. Glue up stock to make wide boards needed for the tops, sides, shelves, dividers, and aprons. Cut all the ¾-

inch-thick parts to size. When you cut the tops, bevel the front edges and both ends at 20 degrees, as shown in the *Top Edge Profile*. **Note:** Glue up the shelf stock from utility lumber, then trim the front edge with a thin strip of primary wood.

Cut four rough leg blanks, about 31 inches long, from the 8/4 stock. Joint two adjacent faces on each blank to make them precisely 90 degrees from one another,

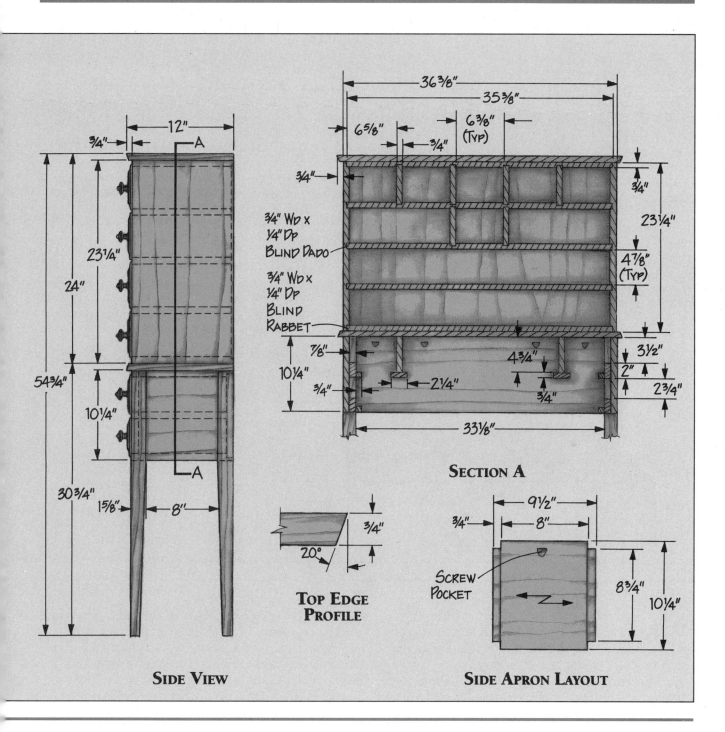

SIDE VIEW

TOP EDGE PROFILE

SECTION A

SIDE APRON LAYOUT

then plane the remaining two faces so the blank is 1⅝ inches square. Cut the legs to length. Cut the remaining 8/4 stock into turning blanks to make the drawer pulls. **Note:** As designed, the apothecary chest requires 26 drawer pulls. If you don't want to turn these yourself, purchase commercially made 1¼-inch-diameter wooden pulls.

2 **Cut the mortises and tenons in the legs, rails, and aprons.** The aprons and rails are attached to the legs with mortise-and-tenon joints. Make the mortises in the legs first, then fit the apron tenons to them.

Lay out the mortises on all four legs, positioning them as shown in the *Front Right Leg Layout*. Each front leg should have a long mortise in one face and three small mortises in an adjoining face. Remember,

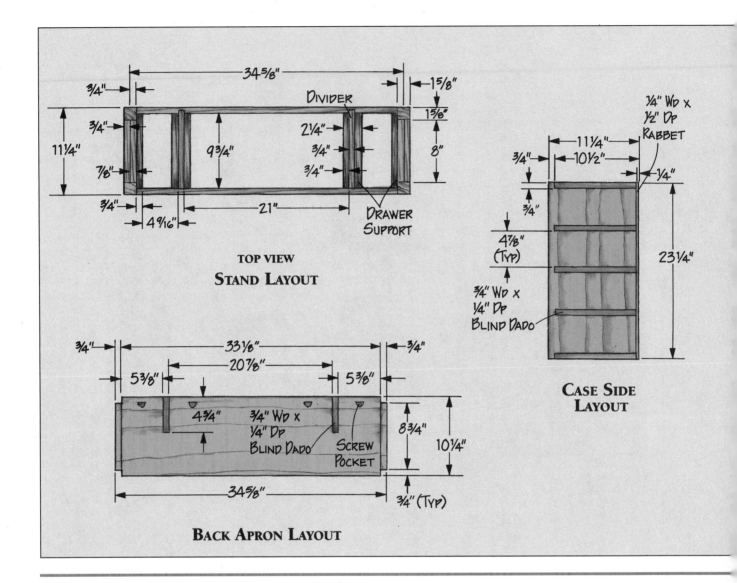

TOP VIEW
STAND LAYOUT

CASE SIDE
LAYOUT

BACK APRON LAYOUT

the front legs should be *mirror images* of each other. The back legs are the same, and each requires two long mortises — one in each adjoining face. Cut the mortises with a router or a drill press.

Cut the tenons on the ends of the aprons and rails, using a dado cutter or a table-mounted router. With a dovetail saw or band saw, cut ¾-inch-wide, ¾-inch-deep notches in the top and bottom edges of the apron tenons, as shown in the *Back Apron Layout* and *Side Apron Layout.*

3 **Taper the legs.** The *inside faces* of the legs are tapered. Make these tapers with a tapering jig on a table saw or band saw. Use a commercially made jig, or cut your own from a scrap of plywood, as shown in the *Tapering Jig* drawing. (*See Figure 8-1.*)

4 **Cut dadoes and rabbets in the sides, shelves, and back apron.** The shelves rest in blind dadoes and rabbets in the sides, and the case dividers rest in blind dadoes in the shelves. The stand dividers rest in blind dadoes in the back apron. Lay out these joints as shown in the *Case Side Layout, Top Shelf Layout,* and *Back Apron Layout.* Note that the bottom surface of the top shelf and the top surface of the upper middle shelf require all four dadoes shown in the drawings. The bottom surface of the upper middle shelf and the top surface of the middle shelf need only the two *middle* dadoes. The other shelves require no dadoes.

Cut the rabbets and dadoes with a hand-held router, then square the blind edges with a chisel. (*See Figure 8-2.*)

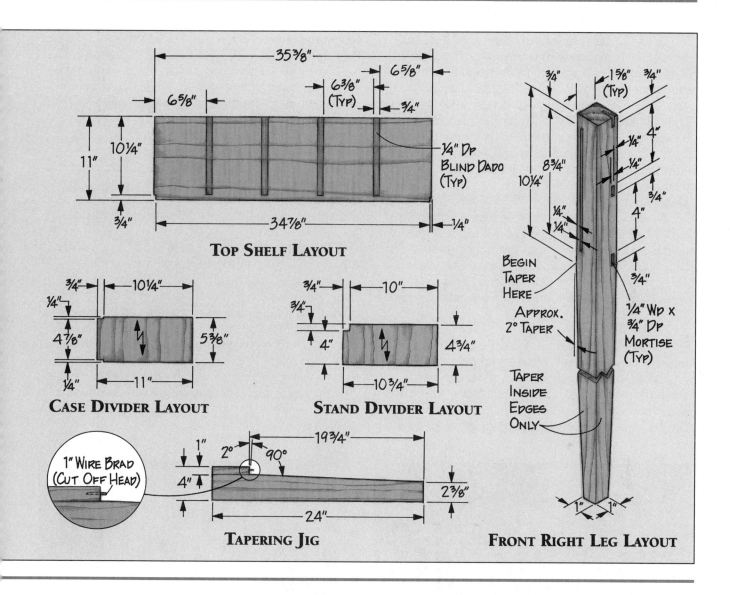

TOP SHELF LAYOUT

CASE DIVIDER LAYOUT

STAND DIVIDER LAYOUT

FRONT RIGHT LEG LAYOUT

TAPERING JIG

8-1 Place the tapering jig on the saw table and fit a leg in it. Tap the top end of the leg with a mallet to seat the bottom end on the wire brads. (The cut-off brads act as claws to help keep the leg in the jig.) Using the fence to guide the jig, push it forward, cutting a taper. Rotate the leg 90 degrees and repeat, cutting the second face. Repeat for the remaining legs. **Note:** Taper the *inside* faces only.

5 **Drill the pilot holes and screw pockets in the top shelf, top rail, and aprons.** The tops are attached to the case and the stand with #8 wood screws. Countersink and drill $3/16$-inch-diameter pilot holes in the top shelf and top rail. Also drill screw pockets with $3/16$-inch-diameter pilot holes in the aprons. *(SEE FIGURE 8-3.)* Since these pilot holes are slightly larger than the shanks of the screws, they will allow the tops to expand and contract with changes in temperature and humidity.

6 **Notch the shelves and dividers.** The shelves and case dividers are notched to fit the blind ends of the dadoes. The stand divider is notched to fit under the top rail. Lay out these notches as shown in the *Top Shelf Layout, Case Divider Layout,* and *Stand Divider Layout.* Cut the notches with a band saw or dovetail saw.

7 **Assemble the stand.** Finish sand the parts of the stand, being careful not to round over any adjoining corners or surfaces. Glue the side apron in the legs and allow the glue to dry. Then fasten the drawer guides to the side aprons with glue and #8 flathead wood screws. Countersink the heads of the screws.

Fasten the outside drawer supports to these guides in the same manner.

Glue the back apron and rails in place, joining the side assemblies. Glue the stand dividers to the back apron and rails. Reinforce the joints by driving screws through the rails and into the dividers. Fasten the inside drawer supports to the bottom edges of the dividers with glue and screws.

Sand all glue joints clean and flush. Then fasten the top to the stand by driving #8 roundhead wood screws through the screw pockets and #8 flathead wood screws through the top rail. Do *not* glue the top in place.

8 **Assemble the case.** Finish sand the parts of the case. Glue the sides, shelves, and case dividers together. Reinforce the glue joints between the top shelf, bottom shelf, and sides with 3d finishing nails, driving the nails through the shelves and into the sides. Sand the glue joints clean and flush.

Fasten the back in place using $7/8$-inch wire brads. Do *not* glue the back to the sides or shelves. Attach the top using #8 flathead wood screws. Again, do *not* glue the top in place. Set the completed case on the stand.

8-2 To rout the blind dadoes in the shelves, sides, and back apron, clamp a straightedge to the stock to guide the router. Stop the router when you reach the blind end of each joint, then square the blind ends with a chisel.

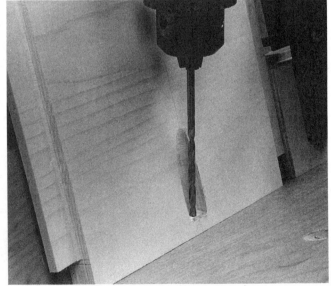

8-3 To make a screw pocket, tilt the drill press table to 15 degrees. Using a fence to hold the workpiece on edge, drill a $3/4$-inch-diameter pocket, then a $3/16$-inch-diameter pilot hole centered in the pocket. The pilot hole should exit the workpiece in the center of the top edge.

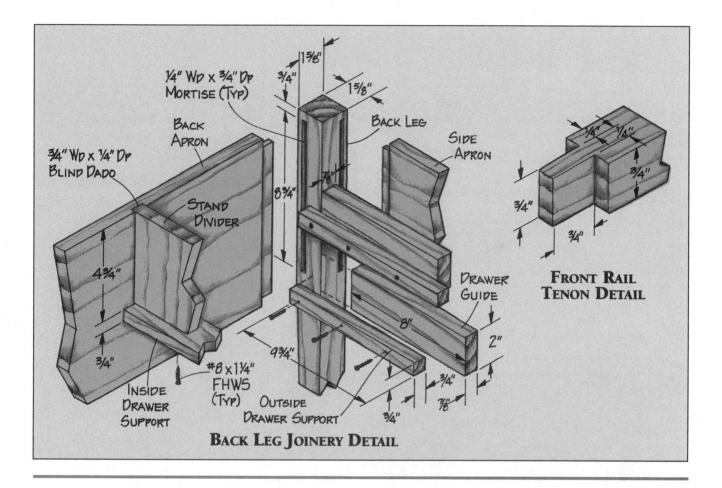

1⅝"
¾"
1⅝"
¼" Wₒ x ¾" Dₚ
MORTISE (TYP)
BACK
APRON
BACK LEG
SIDE
APRON
¾" Wₒ x ¼" Dₚ
BLIND DADO
⅞"
8¾"
STAND
DIVIDER
¼" ¾"
¾"
4¾"
¾"
DRAWER
GUIDE
2"
¾"
8"
¾"
¾"
INSIDE
DRAWER
SUPPORT
#8 x 1¼"
FHWS
(TYP)
OUTSIDE
DRAWER SUPPORT
9¾"
¾"
⅞"

**FRONT RAIL
TENON DETAIL**

BACK LEG JOINERY DETAIL

9 **Cut the drawer parts.** Measure the openings in the case and stand and compare them to the measurements on the drawings. The measurements may have changed slightly — this is normal on a large project. If so, adjust the dimensions of the drawers accordingly. Recalculate the sizes of the drawer parts and cut them.

10 **Chamfer the ends and edges of the drawer fronts.** The ends and edges of the drawer fronts are chamfered at 25 degrees, in the same manner as raised panels. In addition, the medium case drawer front and large case drawer front are shaped to look like several smaller drawer fronts.

Make the chamfers with a table saw. Tilt the blade to 25 degrees and cut all around the perimeter of each drawer front, using a fence to guide the piece. To shape the medium and large case drawer fronts, cut ¼-inch-wide, ⅜-inch-deep dadoes to divide each board into 6⅞-inch-long sections. Bevel the sides of the dadoes at 25 degrees with a band saw. (SEE FIGURE 8-4.)

8-4 To create the divided drawer fronts, first chamfer the ends and edges on a table saw, then cut dadoes in the front to divide them in sections. Bevel the sides of the dadoes with a band saw. The long drawer fronts should look like several small ones.

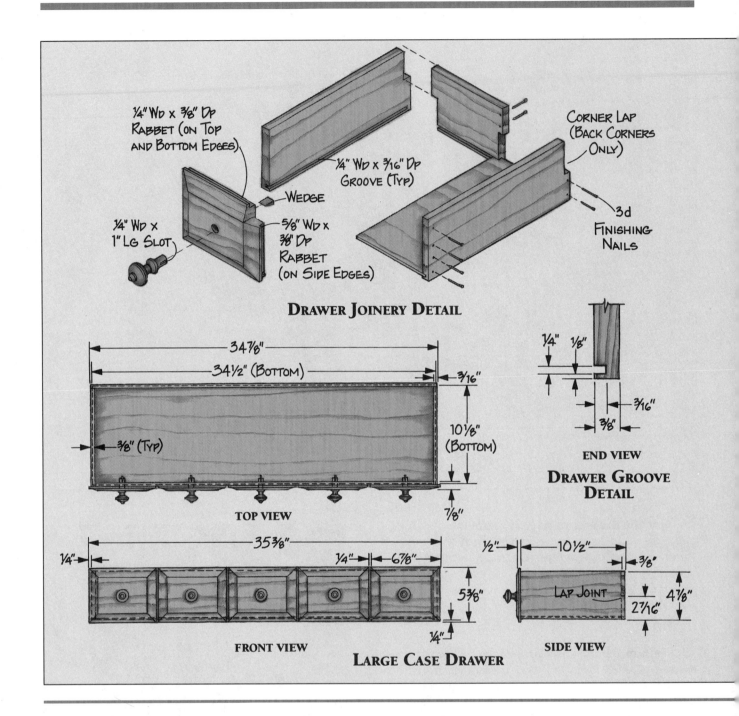

¼" Wd x ⅜" Dp Rabbet (on Top and Bottom Edges)

¼" Wd x 3/16" Dp Groove (Typ)

Corner Lap (Back Corners Only)

Wedge

¼" Wd x 1" Lg Slot

⅝" Wd x ⅜" Dp Rabbet (on Side Edges)

3d Finishing Nails

DRAWER JOINERY DETAIL

34⅞"

34½" (Bottom)

3/16"

10⅛" (Bottom)

⅜" (Typ)

7/8"

TOP VIEW

¼"   ⅛"

3/16"

⅜"

END VIEW

DRAWER GROOVE DETAIL

35⅜"

¼"   ¼"   6⅞"

5⅜"

¼"

FRONT VIEW

½"   10½"   ⅜"

Lap Joint

4⅞"
2 7/16"

SIDE VIEW

LARGE CASE DRAWER

11 Cut the drawer joinery. As shown in the *Drawer Joinery Detail,* the drawer fronts are joined to the sides by rabbets. The back ends of the sides and both ends of the back are notched so they lap. The drawer bottom rests in grooves in the drawer fronts, sides, and back.

With a dado cutter or a table-mounted router, cut ¼-inch-wide, ⅜-inch-deep rabbets in the top and bottom edges of each drawer front, as shown in the *Drawer Front Profile/Side View.* Then cut ⅝-inch-wide, ⅜-inch-deep rabbets in both ends of each front, as shown in the *Drawer Front Profile/Top View.*

Still using a dado cutter or router, cut ¼-inch-wide, 3/16-inch-deep grooves in the inside faces of the drawer fronts, sides, and backs. These grooves should be ⅛ inch from the bottom edges, as shown in the *Drawer Groove Detail/End View.*

Switching to a band saw, cut 2 7/16-inch-wide, ⅜-

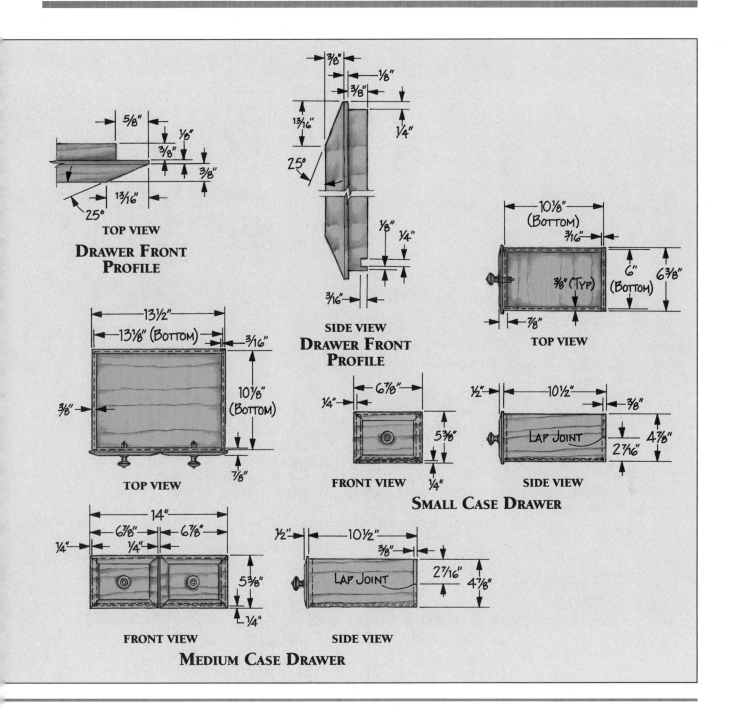

TOP VIEW

DRAWER FRONT PROFILE

SIDE VIEW

DRAWER FRONT PROFILE

TOP VIEW

TOP VIEW

FRONT VIEW

SIDE VIEW

SMALL CASE DRAWER

FRONT VIEW

SIDE VIEW

MEDIUM CASE DRAWER

inch-deep notches in the case drawer sides and back, and 2-inch-wide, 3/8-inch-deep notches in the stand drawer sides and backs. These notches must fit together, forming lap joints at the back corners of the drawers.

Finally, drill 5/8-inch-diameter holes through the drawer fronts for the drawer pulls. (If you're using ready-made pulls, the size of the holes may be different.)

12 Turn the pulls and cut the wedges. If you've elected to make the pulls, turn them to the shape shown in the *Drawer Pull Detail*. With a band saw, cut a 1/4-inch-wide, 1-inch-deep slot in the pull shaft. Then cut wedges to fit the slots.

13 Assemble and fit the drawers. Finish sand the drawer fronts, and lightly sand the other drawer parts. Glue the fronts, sides, and backs together, slid-

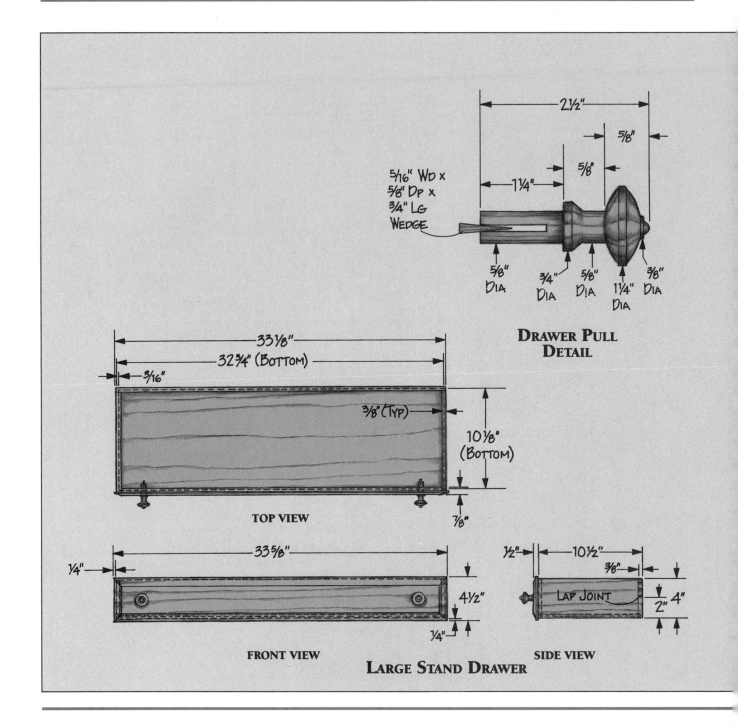

5/16" WD x
5/8" DP x
3/4" LG
WEDGE

**DRAWER PULL
DETAIL**

TOP VIEW

FRONT VIEW   SIDE VIEW

LARGE STAND DRAWER

ing the bottoms in place as you do so. Do *not* glue the bottoms in their grooves; let them float. Reinforce the glue joints with 3d finishing nails. Set the heads of the nails, and sand the glue joints clean and flush.

Glue the pulls in their holes. To make sure they don't come loose, tap the wedges into the slots in the shafts. Leave the shafts slightly long; do *not* cut them flush with the inside surfaces of the drawers.

As shown in the drawings, the drawers should be precisely the same size as the openings. Because of this, they will be a little too large to slide in and out of the case smoothly. Carefully plane, scrape, or file the outside surfaces and top and bottom edges of the drawers until they work properly.

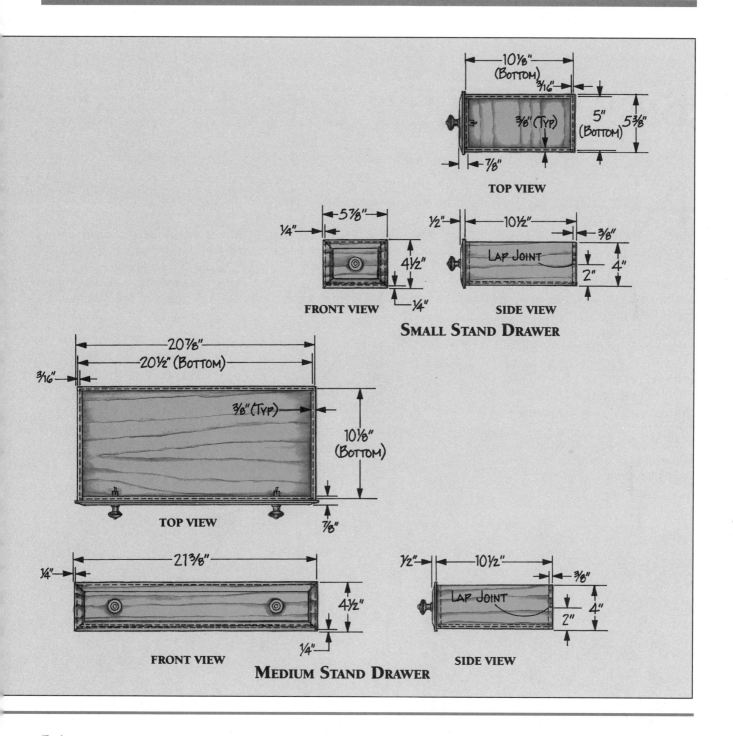

TOP VIEW

FRONT VIEW   **SIDE VIEW**

SMALL STAND DRAWER

TOP VIEW

FRONT VIEW   **SIDE VIEW**

MEDIUM STAND DRAWER

14 Finish the chest.   Remove all the drawers from the completed apothecary chest, marking both them and their openings so you can replace each drawer in the space to which you've fitted it. Also remove the case from the stand.

Do any necessary touch-up sanding to the case, stand, and drawers. Apply a finish to *all* surfaces of the case and stand, inside and outside. This will help keep these assemblies from warping or distorting. Apply a finish to the drawer fronts but *not* to the drawer sides, backs, or bottoms.

When the finish dries, rub it out and buff it with paste wax. Apply paraffin wax to the bottom edges of the drawer sides and backs to help the drawers slide easily. Replace the case on the stand, and the drawers in their openings.

9

BROKEN HEART BOX

Not all boxes are for storing things. There is an interesting category known as *puzzle boxes,* the purpose of which is to confound your every attempt to open them. This heart-shaped box, designed by Tom Lensch of Dayton, Ohio, is one of the most confounding puzzles ever, possibly because it doesn't open like a normal box. The pieces slide apart in three directions, but only if you push on them just right.

The trick is to sandwich the box between your hands, pressing the palms flat against the top and bottom. Twist your hands in opposite directions, rotating the right hand toward you and the left hand away. The parts of the box will slide apart, revealing three small cavities, which, according to Tom, are good for storing almost nothing at all. "Whatever you put in them," he cautions, "is going to fall out every time you open the box."

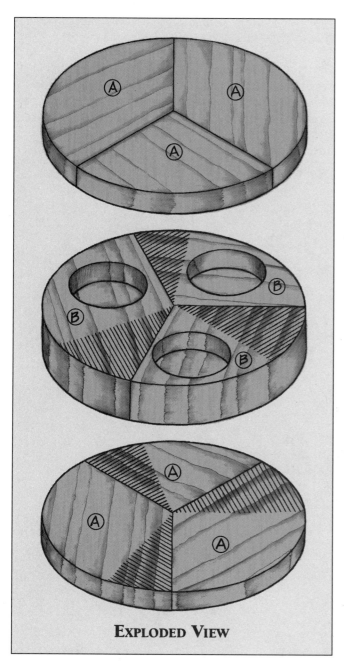

EXPLODED VIEW

PLAN OF PROCEDURE

1 Cut, sand, and finish the wedges. Miter the parts at 30 degrees, creating a 120-degree angle between one edge and the mitered end. Mark a 3-inch-radius arc on each piece, using the point where the mitered end meets the edge as the arc's center. Cut the arcs with a band saw or coping saw.

Finish sand the faces, straight edges, and mitered ends, working your way up to 220-grit sandpaper. Be very careful to preserve the crisp corners. Sand lightly and carefully; you don't want to change the angles or reduce the thicknesses of the wedges too much. Don't bother sanding the curved edges; you'll cut these again later.

Plan how you will join the wedges and where you will apply the glue. On each wedge, carefully mark the areas that will be glued to another wedge. Using an awl, score deep lines in the adjoining faces, dividing the gluing areas from the areas that must slide. (Hereafter, let's call these areas the *glue faces* and *sliding faces*.) The score marks act as tiny troughs, channeling the excess glue away during clamping. Apply a single coat of tung oil to the edges, ends, and sliding faces — the surfaces that will not be glued. The finish helps prevent any glue that does bleed over from sticking to the sliding faces or the adjoining edges. Let the finish dry completely.

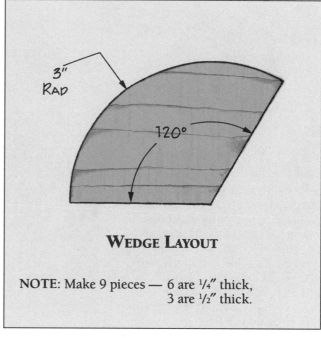

WEDGE LAYOUT

NOTE: Make 9 pieces — 6 are ¼″ thick,
3 are ½″ thick.

MATERIALS LIST (FINISHED DIMENSIONS)

Parts

A. Top/bottom
    wedges (6)   ¼″ x 3″ x 4½″
B. Middle
    wedges (3)   ½″* x 3″ x 4½″

The middle sections may be thicker, if you wish.

2 Glue the bottom and middle layers together.
Arrange the bottom layer of wedges on a scrap of plywood or particleboard so they form a circle. (*SEE FIGURE 9-1.*) Apply a small amount of glue to the glue faces, and place the middle layer on top of the first. The layer of middle wedges must be rotated *30 degrees counterclockwise* from the bottom layer. (*SEE FIGURE 9-2.*) Clamp the two layers together.

Note: Spread the glue as thin as possible; you don't want it to bleed over into the sliding faces when you apply the clamps. Tom applies just 3 or 4 *drops* of glue to each glue face.

3 Glue the second and third layers together.
Let the glue cure for about 30 minutes. Remove the clamps and apply glue to the glue faces on the middle layer. Place the top layer on the middle, once again rotating the upper layer *30 degrees counterclockwise* from the layer immediately under it. (*SEE FIGURE 9-3.*) Clamp the layers together.

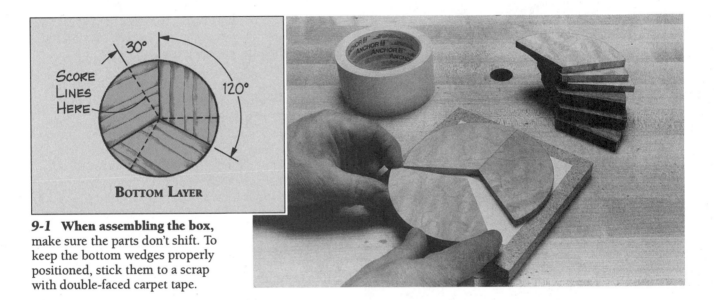

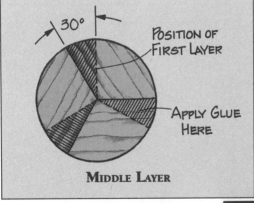

9-1 When assembling the box, make sure the parts don't shift. To keep the bottom wedges properly positioned, stick them to a scrap with double-faced carpet tape.

9-2 Apply glue *very sparingly* to the glue faces of the bottom layer. To keep the wedge layers from shifting as you tighten the clamps, rub together two small pieces of 80-grit sandpaper so that a little grit is sprinkled in the glue. Blow off any grit that drops on the sliding faces. Position the middle layer on the bottom layer, and clamp them together.

4 **Cut the heart shape.** Let the glue dry for another 30 minutes and remove the clamps. Without removing the box from the wood scrap that it's stuck to, mark the heart shape and cut it on a band saw or scroll saw. *(SEE FIGURE 9-4.)* Sand the sawed edges. **Note:** You can cut shapes other than a heart, or leave the box circular, if you wish.

Place the box between your palms and, pressing firmly, twist your hands in opposite directions. The box should slide apart into three pieces. Set the pieces aside and let the glue cure overnight.

Note: You must take the box apart when the glue is only partially cured, just in case some glue has bled over onto the sliding faces. It's a lot easier to break a glue joint before the glue hardens completely.

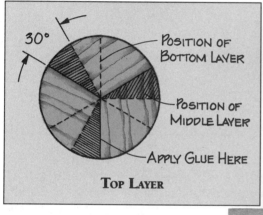

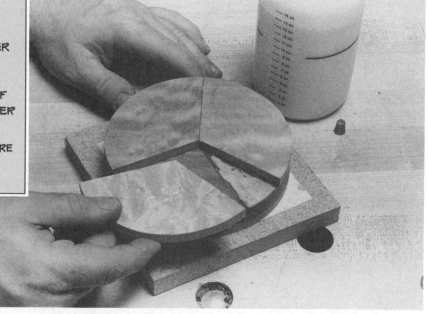

9-3 After the glue sets up between the bottom and middle layers, glue the top layer to the assembly. Once again, use a little sandpaper grit to keep the parts from shifting.

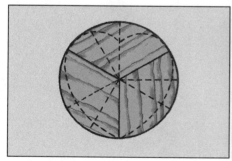

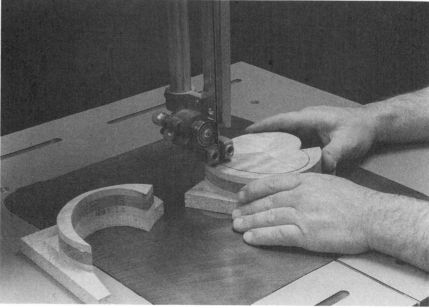

9-4 Cut the shape of the box and sand the edges. To keep the pieces from sliding apart, leave the bottom of the box taped to the scrap while you cut and sand.

TRY THIS TRICK

If the box is hard to take apart, it sometimes helps to tap hardwood wedges between the middle sections, as shown.

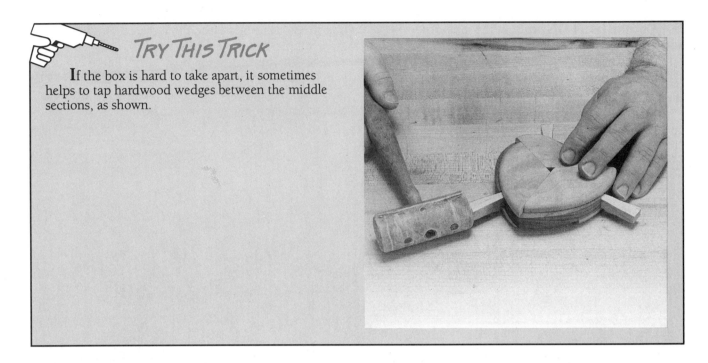

5 Bore the cavities. Using a drill press and a 1³⁄₈-inch-diameter Forstner bit, bore ³⁄₈-inch-deep holes in the top surfaces of the middle layer. *(SEE FIGURE 9-5.)* If you've made the middle layer thicker than ¹⁄₂ inch, bore the holes deeper. Stop them before drilling through to the bottom layer.

6 Finish the box. Do any necessary touch-up sanding, then apply tung oil to all surfaces. Let the oil dry completely and rub it out to make the sliding faces as smooth as possible. Wax and buff the surfaces, then slide the parts of the box back together — if you remember how they fit. (That, too, is part of the puzzle.)

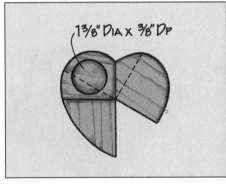

9-5 Slide the pieces of the box apart and drill flat-bottomed holes in the top surfaces of the middle layer. These holes serve as the cavities inside the box.

INDEX

Note: Page references in *italic* indicate photographs or illustrations.
Boldface references indicate charts or tables.

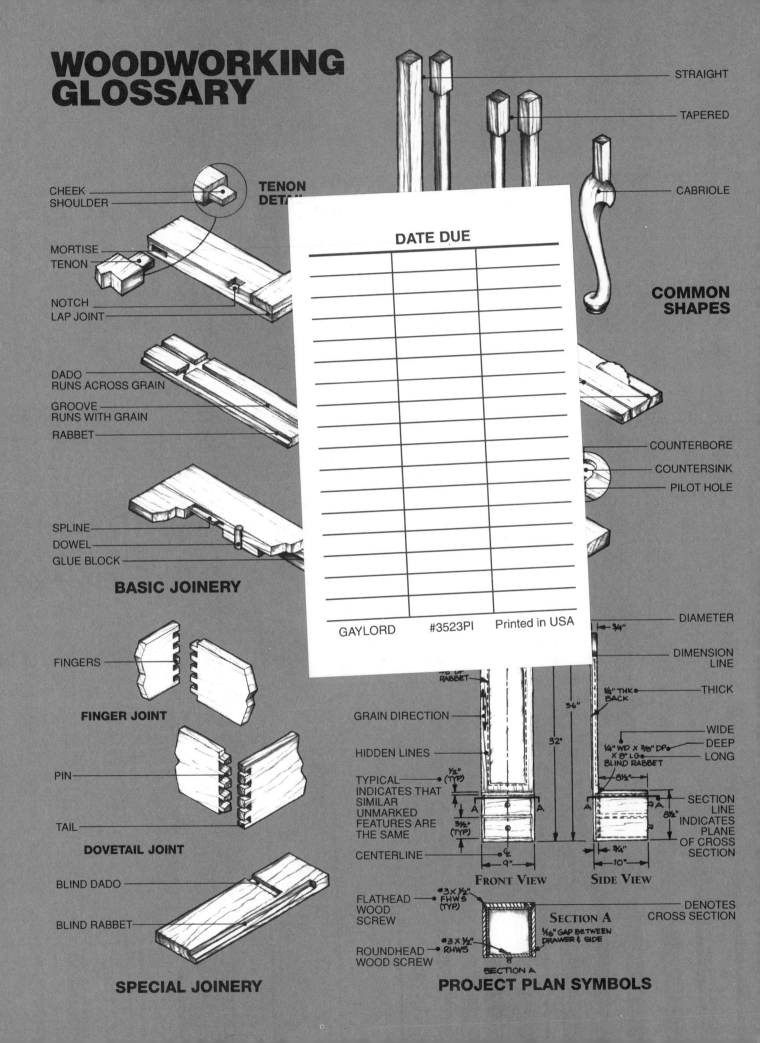

WOODWORKING GLOSSARY

TENON DETAIL
CHEEK
SHOULDER

MORTISE
TENON

NOTCH
LAP JOINT

DADO RUNS ACROSS GRAIN

GROOVE RUNS WITH GRAIN

RABBET

SPLINE
DOWEL
GLUE BLOCK

BASIC JOINERY

FINGERS

FINGER JOINT

PIN

TAIL

DOVETAIL JOINT

BLIND DADO

BLIND RABBET

SPECIAL JOINERY

STRAIGHT

TAPERED

CABRIOLE

COMMON SHAPES

COUNTERBORE
COUNTERSINK
PILOT HOLE

DIAMETER

DIMENSION LINE

THICK

WIDE
DEEP
LONG

SECTION LINE INDICATES PLANE OF CROSS SECTION

DENOTES CROSS SECTION

DATE DUE

GAYLORD   #3523PI   Printed in USA

¾"

¼" THK BACK

36"

32"

¼" WD X ⅜" DP X 8" LG BLIND RABBET

8½"

8½"

¾"

10"

SIDE VIEW

½" DP RABBET

GRAIN DIRECTION

HIDDEN LINES

TYPICAL INDICATES THAT SIMILAR UNMARKED FEATURES ARE THE SAME

CENTERLINE

½" (TYP)

A   A

3½" (TYP)

CL

9"

FRONT VIEW

FLATHEAD WOOD SCREW

#3 X ½" FHWS (TYP)

ROUNDHEAD WOOD SCREW

#3 X ½" RHWS

SECTION A

1/16" GAP BETWEEN DRAWER & SIDE

SECTION A

PROJECT PLAN SYMBOLS